AMAZONIA 1907

AMAZONIA 1907

OUTSIDE THE CIRCLE OF CIVILIZATION

LEE ENGLISH WILLIAMS

FAIR OAKS PRESS • SAN FRANCISCO

For James Orton
of Manchester, England

Published by Fair Oaks Press, San Francisco
Copyright © 2019 by Don E. Roberts
All rights reserved.

Originally serialized in the *New Orleans Times-Democrat* as
*Far from the Beaten Track: Explorations and Adventures of
Lee Williams in the Wilds of South America,* from June 18 to
September 17, 1911. It has been substantially edited and
annotated by Don E. Roberts for publication as *Amazonia
1907: Outside the Circle of Civilization.*

Jacket Art by Michael Mojher

Library of Congress Control Number: 2019938057
ISBN: 978-0-9658811-1-1
A catalog record is available from the Library of Congress.

Manufactured in the United States of America.
Printed on acid-free paper.

Please address inquiries to publisher@fairoakspress.com.

FIRST EDITION

YEARS AGO, I FOUND MYSELF with a couple of stacks of letters, photographs and odd documents that my Alabama ancestors couldn't bring themselves to part with. As the surviving member of my immediate family of four, I had become the latest guardian of fading photographs of unidentifiable faces, wedding invitations and obituaries (those markers of long-ago joys and sorrows), a life insurance policy that covered a life now barely remembered, four ticket stubs for seats in the grandstand of some October 1940 entertainment that my mother wished never to forget, and so on and on. It seemed that nothing had ever been scrapped, but, instead, faithfully transferred from one attic to another over the course of a century.

What appeared to be a folded newspaper, now toasted brown and brittle with age, was four pages clipped from various Sunday editions of the *New Orleans Times-Democrat* in 1911. One of them introduced *Far from the Beaten Track: Explorations and Adventures of Lee Williams in the Wilds of South America,*[1] which was to be serialized that summer; each of the other pages presented a random chapter from the series. The author, Lee English Williams, was the eldest of my grandmother's cousins. He was born in 1875.

I was intrigued by what I read, sometimes with the aid of a magnifying glass. It was the stock-in-trade of authors of adventure stories,[2] but this wasn't fiction. In the introduction to the series, the newspaper had hyped it as "a record of exploration and adventure in the wilds of South America that equals those of Stanley or Livingstone," continuing:

Mr. Williams is not large in stature, but square built, and shows possibilities for immense endurance. Now clean-shaven and healthy, he has an almost boyish appearance, but the time he emerged from the Brazilian jungle he was bearded like a pard and almost as savage looking as the natives themselves.

During the entire journey Mr. Williams made copious notes, and when it was possible, even elaborated his description on the spot, and in every case has understated rather than over-stated his thrilling experiences, which he tells in straightforward, simple style.

If Mr. Williams had entered upon his exploration with a blare of trumpets and with a press agent at work, his exploits would doubtless be familiar to all.

Wondering if, a century later, his exploits were familiar to anyone at all, I turned to two cousins who are more closely related to him than I; he was their grandmothers' brother. One has a hazy memory of having heard of an "adventurer" in the family who was said to have prospected for gold in South Africa, but she knew nothing more.*

By then, my interest was whetted enough to warrant a trip to New Orleans, where what turned out to be fourteen chapters are pre-served on microfilm. The three disconnected chapters had provided a taste of my kinsman's journey: crossing the Bolivian high country on horseback; wandering lost and close to starvation in the Peruvian rain forest; clinging to a raft as it careens through roaring rapids. But the complete narrative proved to be far more than pure adventure, with thoughtful observations of the ancient ways of Perú's secluded Indian tribes and the encroachment of "civilized" men that threatened their existence.

Williams documents his journey in three parts. It begins in the summer of 1906 aboard a ship crossing the South Atlantic to Buenos Aires. In La Paz, Bolivia, he meets James Orton, the Englishman who

---

*In time, I would learn more about Williams and his life, enough to piece together the author's profile on page 159.

will accompany him onward.³ Their goal: "to descend the Amazon from its beginning." The second part follows Williams and Orton to Perú and deep into Amazonia, and this is the heart of his story. In the final chapters, Williams joins a French expedition awaiting the river-boat that will deliver them down the Amazon, back to what he calls "the circle of civilization."

To understand what motivated Williams and Orton, it helps to consider the early years of the twentieth century the beginning of a new Age of Discovery. In 1871, newspaper accounts of Henry Morton Stanley's successful search for the missing explorer Dr. David Livingstone had not only enthralled the American and British public but would fire the aspirations of a generation of boys. Stanley's supposed greeting, "Dr. Livingstone, I presume," was as widely quoted then as Neil Armstrong's "That's one small step for man…" a century later.

Some of those boys would one day become legendary figures in their own right. Sir Ernest Shackleton made the first of his three voyages to Antarctica in 1904. By then, the dull, scholarly journal of the National Geographic Society had become a popular pictorial monthly, and in 1911 the Society cosponsored the expedition that led Hiram Bingham to "rediscover" Machu Picchu. (Four years earlier Williams and Orton had wandered within miles of the sky-reaching Inca citadel, their eyes on the ground.) Then, in 1922, Howard Carter unearthed the treasures of Tutankhamun in Egypt's Valley of the Kings. Lee Williams was of this generation; he, Shackleton, Bingham and Carter were all born within months of each other.

At age eighteen, Williams had gone to sea, to escape what he called "the usual routine" of the life he was expected to pursue. "My sole desire was to see the world, whatever the price may be," he wrote, "Before I was twenty years old, I had visited the United Kingdom and Europe solely by my own efforts. Once the desire to see the strange lands and other people was indulged, the wanderlust⁴ claimed me as a victim." He was thirty-one years old when he arrived in Buenos Aires.

Other outsiders (which is to say, white men) had preceded Williams and Orton into the vast, uncharted Peruvian forests, beginning in the 16th-century with the Spanish conquistadors, followed by missionaries and then various expeditions of geographers, naturalists, archaeologists and seekers of fortune. Of these, I came across only one account of an earlier expedition from Cuzco downriver through the Amazon basin to the Atlantic Ocean. Sponsored by the French National Museum of Natural History in 1846, it was led by Francis de Laporte de Castelnau, who was accompanied by two botanists and a taxidermist.[5] This was six decades before Williams and Orton set off through the same wilderness, unheralded and on their own, with adventure their sole objective. Fast forwarding to the late 1950s, Peter Matthiessen, the American naturalist-writer, directed an expedition from Cuzco that almost perfectly coincided with the route Williams and Orton had followed. But after four punishing weeks and three hundred miles of what turned out to be a wild-goose chase, Matthiessen was relieved to make his escape by airplane.[6]

Williams, expecting the veracity of his story to be questioned, wrote: "I have a passport endorsed by one of the exploration party, that my companion and I came by raft from the Pongo de Mainique, as facts and conditions proved to them that we could have reached that part of the country where we were wrecked by no other means. Those who doubt the actual experiences related in my narrative have but to familiarize themselves with the geography and conditions of that part of the world to be convinced."

Orton anticipated the acclaim they would share upon reaching the Atlantic. But their story was to have quite a different ending, and the sole record of it is this account rendered by Williams and published in the *Times-Democrat* three years afterward.

—Don Roberts

PART ONE

Cape Town to La Paz

Williams arrived in Buenos Aires on April 24, 1906, and resided there for nine months before beginning his northward journey. He sailed from Pará, Brasil, to New York City on August 10, 1908.

1

〰

FTER SIX YEARS of poking about in that world which is, according to accepted impression, described as the Dark Continent and finding that much of its darkness had disappeared—and with it the charm of adventure—I turned my face toward South America.* The doleful blast of the tramp steamer *Surrey*[1] as it gathered impetus for the long journey afforded great satisfaction, for there had been much of hardship and little of profit connected with the years spent in rolling about "east and west of Suez."[2]

The only break in the long voyage from the Cape of Good Hope occurred in the South Atlantic midway between the Cape and the coast of South America in latitude 37° 6' S, at an island of volcanic formation that protrudes much like a gaunt finger, 6,700 feet above the sea. Although twenty miles in circumference, this island, Tristan da Cunha, is a barren, rocky waste, with the exception of a gradually sloping fertile spot, a few miles in area, on the northwestern side.

More than ninety years ago a company of British artillery was stationed there, but was withdrawn a few years later, with the exception of a corporal and one or two companions. The miraculous escape

*He sailed from Cape Town, South Africa, on April 1, 1906.

of members of the crews of unfortunate vessels driven ashore by the fierce winter gales of this lonely stretch of ocean has, from time to time, increased the population. Some of these cast-ups, forming attachments, have settled there permanently, and this accounts for the varied nativity and polyglot language of the present population. The mother tongue of some of the inhabitants is French, of others Spanish or Italian, but the universal language is English.

At the present time, this land, where money as a circulating medium is not used and where all property is held in community, numbers about seventy men, women and children all told. Until about five years ago, every January a man-of-war from the Cape of Good Hope carried supplies from the missionary societies to these people; but after repeated efforts to induce the denizens of this lonely spot to emigrate to Cape Colony, the Cape government, under whose jurisdiction they were, abandoned them to their own resources and the annual visits ceased. Since then they have had no communication with the faraway world except the occasional call of a sailing vessel to take on fresh water.

Barely subsisting on the grain they grow and the cattle they raise, though scourged by terrific southeastern gales during the winter months, they prefer an existence on this extinct volcano, surrounded by a colossal reach of desolate ocean, to a life of more strenuous endeavor on the mainland; not a life of irresponsible ease, provided bounteously by nature, but a precarious existence, at times reduced to dire extremities.[3]

A few years ago an Italian bark was driven ashore near the settlement, and only one of its crew—a mate—escaped the maw of this always-hungry coast. Since this cast-up's unexpected appearance, he has chosen to remain there and fill the place of a much needed benefactor, a schoolmaster. Perhaps the attractiveness of a comely maiden is responsible for this voluntary act of isolation. But his was not the only animal life that escaped from that wreck. Shortly afterwards, rats—heretofore an unknown pest—made their appearance and multiplied so rapidly that they became an ever increasing menace to the food supply of the islands. It was with great difficulty that a sufficient supply of grain could be raised or kept for the season's needs. When this trouble had been lamented to the officers of the man-of-war on one of its annual visits, the resourceful jack-tars[4] on their next visit turned at large about two hundred cats, which they had collected on the mainland. But the remedy proved as distressful as the rat plague. The cats increased to such numbers that they, in turn, caused sore regret, for they destroyed the few fowls that were being bred with great difficulty. At the time of our call to let off a missionary and his wife who had accepted the call to minister to the welfare of the islanders for three years, it was said that the cats had deserted the settlement, had grown wild and had to be hunted in the almost inaccessible rocky sides of the volcano crater. So stupendous an undertaking was the extermination of this steadily increasing cat plague that it was a sorely perplexing question whether the continued multiplication of these animals would not accomplish what the Cape government had so urgently advised: the abandonment of the island.

In their frail, open sailing boats, the hardy islanders sometimes venture for days out of sight of land searching for a possible passing vessel to barter fresh beef and vegetables for tea, salt, ammunition and other simple necessities. To them the appearance of a sail is an eventful day in their lives. Visions of creature comforts are uppermost in their minds.

There seems no likelihood of ever diminishing the supply of fish and sea birds. As our vessel lay head-on under slowly working propeller in the leeward shelter of the island, on account of lack of anchorage depth, countless numbers of albatross circled overhead—some so near that they were killed on the wing with revolvers. Forward on the forecastle deck, off-watch sailors were hauling out fish as fast as a baited tackle could be thrown overboard and drawn in. Some were using lines with two hooks and catching two fish every haul-in.

Probably with a sufficient number of hooks attached, more fish would have been hung than the line would have landed.

An offer of some books to an islander was declined with "Books, books, we have boxes of books yet unopened. Tell the missionaries to send clothing. See these makeshifts—a pair of rawhide moccasins— I haven't had a pair of shoes in years." A letter I entrusted to a resident of the island with instructions to have it mailed by someone on the next passing vessel, reached its destination in Alabama two years after it left my hands.[5]

Two other islands are in the vicinity. The one known as Inaccessible Island, twenty miles distant, possesses special interest on account of having harbored two sailors who underwent a kind of Robinson Crusoe experience there. As castaways on this desolate island, they suffered many privations and were sometimes reduced to great extremities, though, unlike Crusoe, they had an opportunity of quitting the island during their two years' sojourn and were quite ready to take advantage of an opportunity of leaving on a passing vessel.

As the good ship *Surrey* bore south out of her course and circled Gough Island—the third of the group—shrill, piercing screams from the fog siren awakened the desolate solitude. It was feared that some castaway who might have escaped death there was still lingering to perish more miserably by starvation. Only the raucous cries of sea birds answered the awakening echo, and careful scrutiny of the prominent points failed to reveal any sign of human beings.

THE DAWN of the twenty-third day out from the Cape showed the roads of Montevideo,[6] where transfer was made to a night riverboat for Buenos Aires, the queen city of the south.[7] The trip up the river to Buenos Aires was without incident, but there was a babel of tongues and confusion almost without end when the customs officials were encountered at the gate of this modern city. By patience and courtesy the officials finally overcame the linguistic deficiencies of the

14

English-speaking passengers, smug in their self-conceit and apparently laboring under the belief that all the world should know the "mother tongue." That they knew little other than English was made clear, and it was also demonstrated that a little knowledge, even when applied to language, is a dangerous thing at times. An English-speaking woman who became irritated over the manner in which her many belongings were handled by a porter and, realizing the utter futility of urging him by signs and Spanish nouns, resorted to Spanish adjectives. Her mistaken choice of words was more impressive than ladylike and, instead of hurrying the porter, had quite the opposite effect. His dawdling activities came to an end, and he stood wide-eyed and open mouthed until the woman gave up in despair.

The beauty and wealth and gaiety of Buenos Aires have been described by unnumbered visitors, but only those who have stood within the circle of its seductive charm can understand fully the part it plays in the life of the Latin American and why no city on earth save Paris, that other city of enchantment, seems worthy to be compared to it. After nine months of drinking in the charms of this city, where romance and beauty blend so wonderfully with business and enterprise, I encountered quite by chance two fellow countrymen— Roy and Mealey—who were making preparations for an extended tour across the Andes into Northern Bolivia. It required little persuasion to make me one of the party.*

IN SOUTH CENTRAL ARGENTINA, where pack and saddle animals were purchased for the expedition, I saw for the first time the South American cowboy, and a unique figure he presented. His animal was adorned with a silver-mounted bridle, which cost at least fifty dollars, and his bare feet were thrust into solid silver stirrups. A glittering knife, almost sword-like in its proportions was swung across

*They departed Buenos Aires on January 10, 1907.

15

his back, and silver ornaments tinkled upon the reins in his hands. But in horsemanship, dexterity and rope work, he is far inferior to the average cowboy of the American West.

We went on by rail to Rosario,[8] the second city in population and commercial importance in Argentina, and from this point the monotonous journey to Tucumán began. Shortly after leaving Rosario, we encountered immense swarms of locusts. Disturbed by the passing train, they rose in great clouds and the density of the mass was such as to even obscure the sun. As the train carried a dining car and day coaches, in addition to the car containing our animals, we suffered little discomfort until near nightfall, when we reached an alkali desert. With all the windows closed to shut out the dust, the heat in the coaches had become stifling. In a short time, the water supply on the train was exhausted and, within an hour, irritated by the fine dust that filled the coaches, we were suffering intensely from thirst. Finally, when the train stopped momentarily at a little sun-baked hamlet, succor came in the shape of a native woman who offered melons for sale. In the rush, the social status of all on board was reduced to a common level. These melons, which looked much like the cantaloupe of North America, have a sticky quality that should recommend them to those engaged in the manufacture of glue. It was impossible to wipe the juice off our hands and chins, and not until we reached the terminus of the broad-gauge railroad could we rid ourselves of the substance.

Tucumán is the center of the sugar industry in Argentina, with French, English and native capital having established twenty-two mills in the district.[9] Narrow streets and the absence of sanitary improvements are scarcely compensated for by a majestic cathedral and a central plaza of goodly proportions. Throughout South America, the impression seems to be universal that a gringo is an object of legitimate prey. However, familiarity with the language and customs does much to overcome the greed of the native traders and renders business

CHAPTER 1

dealings less vexatious. Two men were required to assist in transferring our animals and equipment to the corral of the narrow-gauge railway. To obtain this assistance we indulged in two hours of bargaining. Each and every native, aided and abetted by the onlookers, attempted to obtain much more than a reasonable amount for his services. It seemed for a time that an agreement would never be reached, but finally an offer of ten pesos, about $4.40, secured the condescending services of a man and a boy. The original price fixed by the applicants was fifty pesos, or about one dollar a minute. The native employer pays about a dollar for four days' work. In dealings with the shop-keepers, laborers or hotels, there is no fixed price, the idea being to obtain as much as possible from each customer.

From Tucumán, our animals were shipped by freight, and in order to feed and water them, we secured permission to travel on the same train. Repeated inquiries at the station failed to elicit any information as to the time of departure. "Mañana," the station agent replied, meaning that it might be a few minutes or a few hours. We waited an hour, at which time there was no indication of the train's leaving, and we questioned the agent once more. "Ten o'clock is the probable hour" was his reply this time. It was then eight o'clock, so we decided to give heed to the cravings of hunger, as we had taken no food since early morning coffee and bread. Returning from the restaurant, we learned upon consulting with the agent that the train had been placed on the mañana schedule once more, so we decided to sleep. Requesting the agent to arouse us in the event that the train did get under way, we rolled up in our blankets and slept until daylight. The train was then on the point of departure, and in a short time the long climb to Jujuy began.

All day and well into the night it was up, up the foothills of the Andes, through an almost uninhabited country. Hills covered with a stunted growth of trees met the horizon on all sides. At intervals the engine came to a standstill for fifteen or twenty minutes in order to accumulate a full head of steam before attempting to negotiate a particularly steep grade. Again under way, the train made rapid progress until the grade was encountered. Then the speed diminished at an alarming rate, and the reports of the exhaust became labored and lengthy. "Will she get over?" was on every lip, and there was always a sigh of relief when the announcement "She is over" was made.

After twenty-three hours of labored puffing the train finally reached Jujuy.[10] There we gained another insight into the character of the native. In making preparations for unloading the animals, it was discovered that the platform used for bridging the space between the car door and the entrance to the corral was missing. Such a platform had never been furnished said the agent, and he added that he did not think one was needed. He insisted that the animals could easily jump the intervening space and made it clear that he had no intention of assisting in the work of unloading. When we would not sign the waybills until the animals were unloaded, he became angry and went off in search of an officer to force us to vacate the car.

Following the disappearance of the agent in quest of the police, one of the laborers about the depot suggested that two pesos, judiciously invested, might result in bringing the platform to light. This sum was tendered and the platform was brought forth without further delay. Upon the arrival of the agent with the chief of police, the former insisted that the animals would then have to be removed from the corral at once, but the representative of the law said that such a ruling would be unjust and it was decided that the corral could be used until another consignment of animals arrived. As such a shipment might not arrive for months, this was entirely satisfactory to us.

Preparations then began for the journey we knew would be full of hardships. Three experienced men were needed: a guide and two pack attendants. We let our desires be known, but applicants were few and far between, not many of the natives caring to risk the dangers and endure the hardships that the positions entailed. After much persuasion, three men agreed to accompany the party. One, a half-breed Indian of North Argentine, consented to attend the animals, and an Andean Indian was accepted as guide. The third man was an English-speaking German, who joined the party because the journey promised to satisfy his love of adventure. (It might be added, in passing, that he obtained his fill of this before the real adventures began.)

We decided to purchase two additional horses as prevision against accidents and were besieged by scores of horse owners, each possessing an animal that was "without a flaw." Nine out of ten of these perfect animals proved to be spavined, wind broken, hip shot or ready to expire of old age. For a solid week we reviewed a parade of broken-down animals before finally securing two that seemed to be reasonably sound.

Altogether, we spent nineteen days in Jujuy, a city from which one could see the snow-capped Andes, the highest peak towering fully 16,000 feet above the level of the sea. The town contained several very imposing churches, but its chief hotel was a thing to rejoice over only when the hour of departure arrived. Instead of the usual morning coffee, we were served maté, the provincial substitute. This is a tea brewed from the leaves of a small indigenous plant. In the humbler homes of the province, maté is said to be one of the chief sustenances of a people who eat very little bread. Its nourishing qualities are such that a small quantity taken at early morning will sustain one until the midday breakfast. It has a delicious aroma and is unquestionably more refreshing than Oriental tea. Even in the humblest homes it is served in ornamented silver cups. A fresh brew is made for each member of the family and is sucked through a silver tube that accompanies the little pot.[11] Ignorant of the etiquette of maté drinking, I inadvertently curtailed my privileges within one family circle by murmuring thanks when served with my first pot. Had I kept silent I would have been offered a second brew, but having expressed thanks and thereby indicating, according to their custom, that no more was wanted, I was not served a second time.

After the nineteenth day, having completed all arrangements, we turned our backs on Jujuy and started off on the eastern bank of the Río Grande. After going about twelve miles we crossed the stream and entered the Humahuaca Ravine.[12] About an hour's ride from the ford, we observed someone standing on a distant hillside, gesticulating and calling out in an excited manner, but as he did not approach we continued on our way. In a few minutes we were overtaken by a very indignant and almost breathless individual who, with insolent sputterings, ordered us to face about and return to Jujuy. When he became less incoherent, we learned that he was the government stock warden and that it was his duty to examine all certificates of ownership.

Advised finally of what the man wanted, we lost no time in producing our documents and offering them for examination, but he would have nothing to do with them. He declared that we had treated his high office with contempt and that we must return and have a hearing at the hands of the officials in Jujuy. After a heated argument, we found him immovable in his purpose to force us to turn back, and, rather than do this, we added insult to injury by driving on. We left him standing in the middle of the highway bringing down the curses of high heaven upon our heads and angry enough to remove those heads instantly if he had been possessed of the power. Our papers were correctly made out and we had received assurances from the Jujuy officials that we would not have to present them until we reached the border.

The hillsides along the Humahuaca Ravine were dotted with Indian barley patches, and these patches were the nearest approach to vertical farming to be found on this round earth. It almost made one dizzy to contemplate their tilted expanse, and I wondered how the farmers kept from tumbling and carrying the crops with them as they rolled downward.

About five o'clock in the evening a halt was called at a farmhouse and the animals were placed in an enclosure containing an abundant growth of weeds and a few tufts of alfalfa grass. The negotiations attending this disposition of our stock were carried on with a woman, the head of the house being absent at the time. When he returned, he expressed great dissatisfaction with the arrangements and attempted, in true Indian fashion, to extort a much larger sum. We refused to pay and were ordered to get out. We declined to do this, and the situation had become quite tense before the Indian finally agreed to a compromise.

The celebration of the native Mardi Gras was to begin the next day* and continue for two or three days, or perhaps longer, since it was the custom to prolong the holiday whenever the people were so inclined.[13] A tom-tom is indispensable on these occasions, and it so happened that our host had made a new one. He was delighted beyond measure with the achievement and remained up all night thumping and adjusting this instrument of torture. He succeeded fully in making us regret that we had not obeyed his injunction to get out.

It rained throughout the night and the following day, and the river attained such a height that we found it impossible to cross. Thus, for two days, we became unwilling guests. However, the celebration of Mardi Gras made our condition endurable. We seemed to be in the center of the affair, natives coming to this point from far and near in spite of the rain and slush. Indeed, the condition of the weather seemed to be of no concern to them. They were out for a good time and were not disposed to let anything interfere with their plans.

The participants in the festivities came mounted, riding from hut to hut and maneuvering for first place at a horizontal pole fixed between two uprights. Those able to retain the desired position for even a short time were entitled to a favor of *chicha* from the host and to repeated favors as long as they were able to remain on their mount.[14]

*February 12, 1907

Chicha,[15] a mildly intoxicating brew, is the native drink of the Andean Indians. To other races a knowledge of how it is manufactured is usually sufficient to satisfy any desire to indulge. To make the drink, Indian maize is first crushed and then chewed until it is moist. After this, it is allowed to ferment, and this forms the basis of the drink. Men are never allowed to assist in chewing the maize, as it is believed among the Indians that it will not ferment unless it is chewed by the women. On one occasion, while in the home of the better class, I was offered a drink of *chicha* and, by way of inducement, was told that only girls with sound teeth were allowed to chew the maize from which it was made.

At night during the celebration, the chief amusement was dancing. The couples, to the accompaniment of weird chanting in Quechua[16] and the resounding thump of tom-toms, whirled through a series of movements, the main idea, apparently, being to approach one another as close as possible without actually touching. As one couple would become exhausted, another would instantly take its place, and the spirit of the occasion was "On with the dance; let joy be unconfined."[17] Those not actually in the dance were consuming wholesale quantities of *chicha* and domestic wine.

Breeding sufficient sheep and cattle to supply their simple needs, and growing just enough grain to provide food for themselves and their stock, these Indians lead a semi-civilized existence of perfect contentment. They enjoy their numerous holidays to the fullest and are satisfied to live in their own way in the shadow of the eternal hills.

2

⌃⌃⌃

T HUMAHUACA, the last Argentine town on our route,[1] we paid the penalty for having failed to treat the stock inspector with the courtesy due his high office. We had halted abreast of the town, which is in the widest expanse of a valley with formidable foothills reinforced by towering peaks adorned with caps of snow, and Roy and Mealey went into town to arrange for pasturage. They failed to return, and we learned they had been arrested on the charge of insulting the officer we had encountered just after leaving Jujuy. It was an act of presumption for the inspector to stop us, but this made no difference. A fine of fifty pesos, about $22.00, was imposed before they were allowed to go, and this experience taught us that the dignity of the little officials in this country was not to be trifled with.

A most unsatisfactory rest was taken there. The scarcity of fuel limited our campfire strictly to cooking, and we were decidedly uncomfortable, the cold having increased perceptibly as we approached the plateau. Breaking camp, which had been pitched below the town, we proceeded along the riverbed only a short distance before our progress was halted and we were given another example of how justice is administered in this valley. "Señores, this Indian says your animals destroyed his corn crop and that you refused to pay for it" was the way we were greeted by the corporal in charge of the soldier-police.

Two of our mules had gotten over the low adobe fence surrounding the Indian's field and eaten a few stalks of corn before being driven out. When the matter was brought to our attention, we offered the Indian five pesos to cover the damage, but the sum was contemptuously declined. Fifty pesos, a sum sufficient to buy the entire crop, was demanded. We refused to pay and the Indian had gone to the authorities with the result that we were once more in the clutches of the law. A full day's time and seventeen pesos were the cost of this experience.

Escape from Humahuaca was followed by a short day's ride, a night in the open and then a long, wearisome march of forty miles. At noon we passed Tres Cruces,[2] a point where three natural crosses appear on the mountainside, and shortly thereafter reached Esquina Blanca,[3] the entrance to the plateau. Reaching before us—more than 12,000 feet above sea level—a long stretch of alkali plains extended beyond the border into southern Bolivia.

It was our intention to stop for the night at Abra Pampa, one of the waterholes on our route, but the shades of evening fell before we reached that point. Rain seemed imminent, so hurried preparations were made to spend the night upon the open pampa.[4] We expected a miserable time and were not disappointed. The night began with a tremendous downpour, accompanied by terrific thunder and a dazzling display of zigzag lightning. The wind howling with fierce intensity, the vivid flashes of lightning and the awful crash of thunder filled us with a sense of our utter helplessness. With nothing over us but our ponchos, we crouched close to the ground and waited for the elements to spend their fury, but the storm did not abate until the night was almost spent, and when daylight came, it did not take us long to reach the hut of a sheep herder, about a half mile distant. We cooked breakfast at his hut, and I do not recall eating a more enjoyable meal in all my varied experience.

The next halt under shelter was at Capilla, which derives its name from the house of worship established there.[5] Biennially a parade visits this place for the purpose of holding services, performing church rites and collecting the offerings of the people. As money is practically unknown to this community, contributions of the congregation consist of sheep, goats and burros. We got our first insight into the home life of the Andean Indians there. Crushed barley, cooked in patties or small cakes, and dried goat's meat constitute their diet. They live in adobe huts, which usually have two rooms. One of them is used for storage purposes, while the other does service as bedroom, kitchen, dining room and parlor. The family, the shepherd dogs and such fowls as are on the place make common use of this one room. In every home the most conspicuous utensil is the calabash,[6] a begrimed vessel containing the family water supply. The dogs drink from this along with their masters; members of the family wash their hands and faces in it; and the cook uses it in mixing her meal just as if it were fresh from the clear mountain stream. The cook, usually an old woman, smacks first the dogs and then the children with her ladle and sometimes stirs the pot and dips water with it, indifferent to the stray hairs and ever-present grime.

Sheep and llama wool is spun by the women in a primitive but dexterous manner. They spin the bobbin between the palms of their hands, working away with a patience remarkable to behold. The yarn, thus manufactured, is woven into blankets and cloth on rudely constructed looms. These looms are made of four pegs driven into the ground with crosspieces for holding the lengthwise threads attached to opposite sides. The weaver, seated upon the ground, works the bobbin from side to side, forcing the threads together with a piece of flat wood. The cloth, though coarse and heavy, is of remarkable durability. It is said that a discarded garment made of this cloth is never seen. Once put on, the garment is not removed except under the most extraordinary circumstances. When holiday attire is to be worn, it is put on over the everyday garment. A bath is an almost unknown experience among these people.

From Capilla, we headed due north for the border town across the alkali plain, where vegetation was scant and water very scarce. Mirages of wonderful clearness and beauty were of daily occurrence on this sunbaked stretch. At a distance, in an expanse that more nearly resembled water than land, we could see burros, llamas and sheep grazing peacefully, while near at hand stood the shepherds and the humble huts in which they made their homes. Suddenly the luring picture would vanish, leaving only the shimmering desert.[7] One green spot proved to be real, and it was indeed a grateful find. A slight expanse of turf revealed a small spring from which clear water bubbled to the surface. The overflow moistened the ground for a short distance and then sank again into the earth.

The snow-capped barriers to the east and west receded farther and farther as we approached the border, but were not entirely lost to view until we entered the driest stretch on this plateau. After we had crossed the only stream encountered and ascended a slight elevation, the border post of La Quiaca[8] came into view. It consisted of a collection of adobe structures, the offices and living quarters of the customs officials.

While Roy and Mealey were engaged in showing the officials our permits, a police official approached our pack train[9] and inquired, "Señor, is one of your natives named Suares?"

"Yes, Señor Official, my name is Suares," interposed the guide.

"Come with me, then," said the official.

Mealey and I followed the prisoner to the office. In reply to our questions, the arresting officer said, "Señores, I have instructions from Jujuy to detain your party and recover a mule branded 'J.E.,' and place the Indian under arrest for its theft."

There being no such mule among our lot, Mealey asked the Indian to explain.

"Yes, señor," the Indian replied, "I took the mule from the pasture because the owner owed me eighty pesos and refused to pay."

"Where is the mule?" asked the official.

"Señor, I owed a man and I gave it to him," replied the Indian.

It was very clear that the Indian did not realize he had broken a law, either moral or statutory. No description of the Indian had been furnished the officials at this place, and if our guide had denied his identity, as he probably would have done had he known that in attempting to collect a debt in such fashion he had broken the law, he would doubtless have escaped. As it was, we lost our guide, and a good one he was, too. All efforts to secure another guide to direct us as far as Tupiza proved unavailing, so we decided to cross the border and trust our own resources rather than undergo an indefinite delay.

Half an hour after leaving La Quiaca, we passed the stone pillars marking the boundary line and entered Bolivia.[10] It was with a sigh of relief that we passed into this country, thinking we would probably escape further annoyance at the hands of officials. Our party appeared more spectral than real, passing through an almost barren waste of dunes and deep washouts, man and beast covered with a powder-like dust. To the right, to the left, ahead and behind, undulating stretches of sand hills reached away to the horizon, the only change in the monotony of the scene occurring when we encountered a deep washout, showing where the waters had raged during the rainy season.*

Two days of travel through this country brought us to Mojo, the Bolivian customs station.[11] The officials here proved to be very considerate, and when we left we were given a letter to the agent at Estancia Maria, six miles distant, asking him to provide us with three days' pasture. Inquiring for meat, we were told that it was an unattainable luxury so far as the open market was concerned. "But," said an official, "you will see herds of sheep and goats en route. Don't

*In Bolivia and Perú, the rainy season extends from December through May.

attempt to bargain for one of these, for the owners will not sell. Just shoot one and pay the Indian two bolivianos.[12] He will object, but it is legal."

We remained as guests of the station until late in the afternoon and then saddled for the march to the prospective camp. About two miles from the post, we came upon a herd of goats, and Mealey and I rode among them. We selected one and immediately shot it. The herder came running to us, protested violently and then fled to inform his master. In the meantime, the goat was prepared for packing and placed on the half-breed's horse. He was instructed to ride on and prepare a meal while we remained on the spot to await developments.

In a very short time three angry Indians, armed with stones and knives, appeared. When they were near enough to see, I held up a gold coin to let them know we were willing to pay for the goat. This quieted them until it was discovered that there were not two bolivianos in change among the party. The Indians became suspicious over the delay and began to jabber excitedly and point in the direction of the customs station. It finally dawned on us that they wanted us to go back to the station and settle with them under official supervision. We objected to this and, holding up three fingers, said, *"Maria, Maria,"* to let them know that if they would accompany us to our camping place, we would give them three bolivianos. They would not consent to this, and finally Mealey decided that returning with them to the station was the only means of disposing of the difficulty.

Mealey had gone only about a mile with the Indians when they were joined by others and the entire crowd attacked him. He wheeled his horse and dashed for our party as rapidly as possible, leaving them behind. He had just reached us when we saw a man approaching, riding rapidly and recklessly. "Señores, I am the chief police official. You will please return to Mojo. You are charged with theft and assault," he announced as he drew rein. Explanations were offered and a sovereign[13] was tendered and accepted in payment of four bolivianos for the goat, the value of which having increased at an alarming rate.

"Señores, I have no change with me, but I will send the eight bolivianos and sixty centavos to your camp," he promised when the money was passed over. Having received an acknowledgment in writing, we proceeded on our journey.

Estancia Maria consisted of the agent's house, a few adobe huts and a police station. We discovered the latter immediately upon our arrival. As we rode up, we were met by two Indians and two soldier-police. The Indians proved to be of the party who had first appeared on the scene after the slaying of the goat. They pointed to Mealey and me, and the officials said, "Señores, you will please accompany us to the police station." Wonderfully polite, those Bolivian officials! By way of enforcing their request, the officials presented their antiquated guns, and we lost no time in complying. The barrel of the weapon that covered me seemed to have a bore as large as a water main. "Hombres," I urged, "please keep the muzzle of your guns pointed up. They might go off and kill one of our animals." This piece of pleasantry fell upon deaf ears. We were escorted to a cobbler's shop, where justice was dispensed, and were told that the charge against us was the theft of a goat. The receipt from the Mojo official was displayed, and this ended the difficulty.

"I have had about enough goat for one day," Mealey declared when we headed for camp, but he changed his mind that night after the ribs of the goat were done to a turn over the coals of the campfire. The following day was devoted almost entirely to eating and sleeping, the exposure and hardships of the trip having left us thoroughly fagged. Protection from the heat of the sun was welcomed by day, but that night it became extremely cold, and we longed for a fire. The scarcity of wood made this an unattainable comfort.

The route to Tupiza began with a steep, winding climb over the first few miles. From the summit of this rise, the Indian village of Nazaret on the Río San Juan was visible.[14] It was not more than three miles away, but the trail route was fully four times as long. The trail led along the edge of chasms of such depth that it made one's head swim to glance downward, and we rode forward with extreme care. A false step would have meant a terrible death in the darkness of the canyon far below.

Recent rains or melting snow had so swollen the stream we were following that it appeared wild and dangerous, but we reached a ford that the guide we hired in Mojo assured us was safe to cross. He led and we followed until we found ourselves forced to swim for our lives, the water being much too deep for the horses. We finally reached the opposite shore after an exciting struggle with the angry waters.

Gold dredging was in operation on this river. Steel-hulled dredges had been transported across the mountains upon the backs of mules and assembled at the scene of operations—one about twelve miles from Tupiza and two others at other points on the river. The measure of success achieved by the promoters of this dredging scheme was a matter of speculation, those engaged in the work being reticent on the subject. That they deserved success, however, seemed certain, for they had overcome obstacles that required not only large capital but stout hearts. Fuel was extremely scarce in this vicinity, but a fair substitute was found in the moss that abounded along the river. Once dried, this moss served very well in lieu of coal or wood.

When we were within seven miles of Tupiza, the trail, which paralleled Río San Juan, became impassable on account of the flooded stream, and we were forced to take the dangerous overhead pass. This led along the face of a cliff, the path gradually ascending until we were a thousand feet above the river. When the trail reached its greatest height, there was no room for animals to pass one another, and it was necessary to send the guide ahead to notify anyone coming from the opposite direction to await our arrival. Then the trail suddenly dropped, forming a kind of spiral stairway. We had made the journey without incident until we reached this point, where the German, who was riding just behind me and in front of Mealey, suddenly wailed, "I am dizzy; I can't go down."

"You *must* go down, so move along," Mealey shouted.

"I shall fall" was the reply of the poor fellow, who was white as a sheet and almost in tears.

"Shut your eyes and hold tight; the mule will carry you down safely," said Mealey.

The animals were becoming restless and the situation beginning to impress us as rather serious when Mealey solved the problem by starting his animal forward. The German had to move then or be crowded from the trail into the dizzy depths below, so he moved, and we reached the bottom.

Across the river at the foot of this path, we found an Indian hut surrounded by a patch of green corn. The sight was too much for our always-hungry pack animals, and before we could check them, they were across the low hedge fence attacking the young corn. With great difficulty we succeeded in getting them out of the lot. We had barely driven the last one across the hedge when the Indian owner appeared, followed by his entire family, and they kicked up a terrific row. A generous number of bolivianos satisfied the indignant family, and we proceeded along the riverbed, shortly thereafter entering the canyon that led into the Tupiza Valley.

Following the riverbed through the valley for a few miles, we came to the outskirts of Tupiza, a city of about 12,000 people.[15] The 36 miles of unusually rough road, combined with the delay caused by the high water, had held up our arrival until considerably past the usual hour for retiring, and our passage through the streets was marked by the appearance of numerous nightcaps in the windows along the way. We went to the Gran Nacional Hotel filled with pleasurable anticipation of comfortable beds and meals of something other than canned goods, of which we'd had our fill during the long days on the trail. But the bed in which I spent the night was infested with *benchucas,* bugs almost as large as cockroaches, and for three days I felt the effect of their onslaught.[16] I must have proven a tough proposition, however, for the bugs did not trouble me again, though I occupied the bed for several nights.

The remarkable ability of Andes Indians when it comes to walking is a matter of unending comment among visitors, and while this subject was being discussed in the hotel one night, the following was related as fact: A mining engineer in charge of some work nearby laid a wager with some doubting new arrivals that one of his servants could go on foot to Jujuy, a distance of 270 miles by trail, deliver a letter to a responsible party there and return with the answer within seven days. The Indian accepted the commission as a mere matter of routine and walked the 540 miles within the specified time without apparent inconvenience.

At Tupiza, the members of our little party were reduced by the desertion of the German. Dr. Soza, an obliging resident of that city who was familiar with the route to Uyuni, our next destination, volunteered to aid us in securing a guide. It was, however, impossible to engage one who was thoroughly satisfactory, and we were finally forced to accept the service of a Quechua who impressed us far from favorably. With great regret, we turned our backs on this charming little city. Its central plaza, where a band played sweet music each night, had proved a pleasing attraction, and the bewitching girls, who promenaded there under the watchful eyes of parents or guardians, added to the delight of the scene.

3

THE ROUTE to Uyuni followed the bed of Río Tupiza at the outset, and some very remarkable formations were observed along this stream. At one point, where the wall on either side was of soft sandstone, the rocks had been sculpted into queer and beautiful forms. Statues and medieval castles stood out as if carved by hand, the turrets of the castles so accurate that one could scarcely realize that they had been chiseled by the onrushing waters. One of these specimens of nature's handiwork standing boldly against the sky instantly suggested the figure of a Dutch burgher attired in frock coat and tile hat, wearing a fringe of whiskers much like those that adorned the face of Oom Paul.[1] These figures were so striking that no one could fail to be impressed with their close resemblance to the works of mankind.

Toward the close of the second day out from Tupiza, as we came to a wide, dry area of the riverbed, the wind, which had been whispering about in grateful little swirls, began rapidly increasing strength and in a little while was blowing furiously. In its mad, swirling flight it picked up great quantities of dust, sand and pebbles, and swept them forward with tremendous force. The dust was blinding, suffocating, and the pebbles beat upon us with such fury that it was extremely painful. Urging the almost maddened animals forward as rapidly as possible, we came upon a cave-like washout where we hurriedly dismounted and protected ourselves and the animals as best we could.

I have passed through some extremely violent sandstorms upon the African veldt, but never before witnessed a storm of such intense fury. The dense cloud of flying particles hid the sun, while the shriek of the wind, together with the rattle of the pebbles, created a roar and din that drowned our voices. In the haste to escape its fury, we failed to hitch our animals upon reaching the cover, and when the storm abated we found that they had run into a nearby pasture, where they mingled freely with cows and burros. They showed no disposition to continue the journey, and it was with difficulty that we finally separated them from the herd and resumed our way.

Shortly after this, we passed a herd of domestic llamas, and our animals stopped stock-still and surveyed these ungainly-looking creatures with evident interest. One of the animals, a frisky mule, whose bump of curiosity seemed unusually well developed, approached too close and was rewarded with a spray of ill-smelling saliva, one of the llamas having brought its defensive batteries into action.

Through a narrow canyon with grim, sky-reaching sides, devoid of vegetation, we entered Oro Ingenio,[2] ending a jaunt of thirty-six miles. During the day we had seen but one evidence of human beings—a dilapidated Spanish smelter, so long abandoned that its builder had no doubt been gathered into the earth from which he had hoped to wring great riches. At Oro Ingenio, the only green thing in sight, outside of a few bunches of alfalfa grass, was some green corn growing about an Indian cabin. By much persuasion the Quechua, our guide, induced the owner to allow us to use a part of the enclosure. Gold was offered in payment, but for some unaccountable reason was refused. All the Indians encountered in this section seemed chary of gold coin, though gold is in general use throughout the country. We had been cautioned concerning this prejudice against the yellow metal and had provided ourselves with some national currency at Tupiza, but the amount procured was not sufficient for the journey. Because the Indians make a practice of hoarding silver coins, it is difficult to secure exchange for gold in this part of Bolivia.

That night I slept under a small tree on an elevated spot near the hut and was greatly surprised to discover at dawn that it was an apple tree—certainly an odd find. I stuffed as many apples as I could into my saddlebags and munched them with great satisfaction as I rode along that day. They were hard and sour and no larger than a walnut, but it had been so long since I had tasted fruit that they were as delectable as golden russets.

Early in the morning, the Quechua begged permission to saddle his mule and go to the chapel, about a quarter of a mile distant, for the purpose of worshiping, but when he reached the chapel, he continued to ride and we knew he had deserted us. We decided that it was useless to attempt to overtake him, for, if caught and brought back, he would desert again at the first opportunity. Moreover, we were out nothing, as he was to be paid when we reached Uyuni.

On one occasion while residing in Africa, I inquired of the Zulu outdoor servant concerning the whereabouts of the houseboy, the hour being late and the lad not about his duties.

"He no wash he face, bass," was the enigmatic reply.

On further questioning, the Zulu said, "He Basuto, bass; no want money; he go home."[3] In other words, the privileges of a reasonably well-kept house, together with fair compensation, were not to be weighed against the attractions of home, and the houseboy had fled. This trait of the African is keenly developed in the Andean Indian. He works, as a rule, only because his master forces him to do so, and if circumstances are such as to make escape possible, he will desert when the lure of home becomes too strong.

At this stage of the journey we began to be impressed with the fact that the Andean Indian's knowledge of measured distance was about as vague as his knowledge of the white man's religion. He reckons distance by the time it takes his fleet feet to cover it and is utterly at sea when any ordinary standard is introduced. At Tupiza, Dr. Soza furnished us with a list of *tambos,* or halting places,[4] and the probable distance between each. All efforts to implement this information by inquiring among the Indians we met along the way proved discouraging. The following bits of conversation were typical of many:

"How many leagues to the next *tambo?*" we asked.[5]

"Don't know, señor," the Indian replied.

"Is it three leagues?" This by way of suggestion.

"Yes, señor."

After a ride of two hours, another Indian is met. "How far to the next *tambo?*" he is asked.

"Don't know, señor."

"Is it as much as four leagues?"

"Yes, señor."

Never to disagree with a white man seems to be a characteristic of these people.

We were now without a guide. From Oro Ingenio our march continued through the canyon, and for mile after mile the towering walls held us in their close embrace, until the trail ascended sharply and brought us among the everlasting snowcaps upon a plateau. At a *tambo* at Encoriani[6] where we spent a night, I slept for the first time upon a heated stone bed. These beds are constructed with a hollow space beneath, enclosed on all sides with but two small openings— one for inserting fuel for fire and the other allowing smoke to escape. When the stranger arrives, shivering from the intense cold of this altitude, a sagebrush fire is built and kept burning throughout the night. Under this treatment the stones become just warm enough to be grateful to the touch of limbs that have become numb with cold, but by no flight of the imagination can the stones be made to feel soft, and unless the traveler is unusually well provided with bedding, he is very likely to awake with a feeling of "all hips" after a night on one of these beds. The houses in which the stone beds are used have openings designed to facilitate the escape of the smoke that constantly arises from about the sleeping guest's feet, but the scheme of ventilation is open to improvement, and, as a rule, we awoke in a dull stupor from breathing the smoke-laden air.

Each day now became more nerve wracking, and the lack of a regular supply of food caused the animals to act with accentuated stubbornness. They developed a decided disinclination to keep to the trail, and it was with growing difficulty that we moved forward. Shortly after leaving Encoriani we encountered a poison weed; we had been informed that this grass was certain death to animals. Despite the fact that the trail made a wide detour, this invitingly green grass was in plain view, and it was almost impossible to keep the hungry animals from bolting forthwith. With relief we finally left the green spots behind.[7]

We camped one night in the bed of a ravine in which we had traveled a great part of the day, choosing a spot hemmed in on one side by vertical cliffs and on the other by sand dunes and washouts. Beginning at dark, the clouds, which had become more threatening as the day advanced, were split by brilliant shafts of lightning, and the rain descended throughout the entire night. In the morning we found that our animals had broken away and become separated. While engaged in the search for them, I noticed a small fox-like creature[8] and took a shot at it with my revolver, much to the horror of the half-breed who was with me. The shot went wild, and, according to the half-breed, my luck in escaping death on this journey was due to this fact. Even the *attempt* to kill the animal would be fraught with dire consequences, he declared, and before the day was over he had occasion to say "I told you so."

When finally located, my horse eluded every effort to place the bridle upon him, and I finally saddled one of the horses bought in central Argentina instead. About two hours after breaking camp, as I urged this horse into a canter along a level stretch, he stumbled. I jerked my feet from the stirrups but he turned a complete somersault and came down with the weight of his hips across my legs. The half-breed instantly reminded me of the prediction he had made when I fired on the fox, but he condescended to assist Mealey in pulling the animal off me. A slight sprain of the right knee was the only injury I suffered, and I was inclined to count myself lucky rather than unfortunate.

Shortly before sighting Tambo Tambillo,[9] we reached the highest point on this route, an altitude of about 15,000 feet. Here we encountered a snowstorm of short duration, which was followed by hail. The wind whipped the hail into our faces with such force that the animals turned their heads leeward and refused to about-face until the storm abated. At Tambo Tambillo we were greatly surprised and immensely gratified to find both fresh meat and potatoes. Later we learned that this welcome change was because the following day was to be devoted to the celebration of a church holiday, and these luxuries had been provided for the occasion. Under the influence of generous hospitality, we treated the natives from our scant supply of sugar and tea with reckless prodigality. Then the stone beds were heated, the corral gates securely fastened, and we slept the sleep of complete fatigue. I had been sleeping but a few minutes, it seemed, when the half-breed called, saying that coffee was ready and it was time to depart. As we mounted, the gray mist of dawn enveloped us in a chilly embrace, and it was with reluctance that this halt was ended.

The route from Tambo Tambillo wound uphill and down, through an almost endless expanse of brown hills, reinforced by great peaks whose crests were capped with the snow of ages—great white caps on an ocean of hazy blue that reached as far as the eye could follow. The only sign of life was an occasional llama or burro pack train, or, perhaps, a herd of scampering vicuña, the most timid of all Andean animals. The crumbling ruins of long-since abandoned smelters, mute tokens of the Spanish lust for gain, were encountered daily now. Most of these were in such a state of collapse that, when seen at a distance, they seemed mere heaps of stone. At what appeared to be an important junction, we halted at a *tambo* where corral and forage, sweet

38

bread and eggs were available. This indicated that something of a white-man's civilization was near at hand; the Indians provide no such luxuries for their own convenience or gratification.

The trail again was taken up. We made a gradual ascent and at noon were able to see the Bolivian city of Uyuni from the summit of the last elevation, the distant prospect arousing our anticipation of sweet bread and eggs.

Uyuni occupies a position on a wind-swept plateau, 12,000 feet in elevation, that stretches away to Lake Titicaca.[10] We approached by a sharp descent and, after traveling for two hours across the plain, saw a train speeding over the level expanse, leaving a trail of smoke behind it—surely a remarkable sight to a party of trans-Andean adventurers after so many days spent out of touch with modern thought and progress. The most noticeable sight on entering Uyuni was the great number of pack trains of llamas and burros, either in motion or waiting to load or unload. The narrow-gauge railroad from Antofagasta, a Chilean seaport, passes through Uyuni en route to Oruro, the Bolivian terminal, and this makes the town an important distribution point for the immediate surrounding territory. It is said that this railroad is the best-paying proposition of its kind in South America. I noticed a novel scheme for propelling handcars upon the rails: When the wind is fair, a sail is hoisted upon the car just as if it were a boat, and away this strange-looking landcraft hurries.

Only a few stops, chiefly at stations where mines were located, marked our journey by rail from Uyuni to Oruro,[11] a trip of about twelve hours. Extraordinary activity in the latter city proclaimed the presence of Americans engaged in railway and mining enterprises on the plateau. An effort to put the railway through to La Paz within the time fixed by the contract had awakened this town to such a state of hurry and bustle that the natives seemed almost stunned by the display of energy. The tremendous determination and tireless labor of these American railroad builders, with their modern methods and energetic enterprise, presented a glaring contrast when viewed in the light of Andean Indian ways.[12] Contented with the tools of his fore-fathers, the Indian breaks the soil with a wooden plow and performs with his bare hands the work that machinery does for the white man in a fraction of the time. Railroads? He has no use for them. The travel lust has not developed in him, and when necessity calls him to some distant point, he can travel as far in a day, bearing his pack all the while, as any animal would travel in the same length of time. But there is gold, tin, silver and copper in this country, and the white man has come to dig it from the earth and carry it away. In doing this, he is building railroads and carrying on great schemes of indus-trial development, but if he is injecting enterprise into the Indian character, it is by a process so slow that the observer fails to detect it.

In Oruro we became acquainted with the manager of a local branch of an American financial institution and were invited to spend an evening at his home. We accepted and during the evening our host-ess brought forth some homemade chocolate candy—the first I had seen since leaving my home in America, nearly seven years before. The brown sweets resurrected memories of long ago, and for the first time in many months, I felt the pang of homesickness, that melan-choly affliction to which no one ever becomes entirely immune. Moreover, the impressions of our journey through yawning gorges, across alkali plateaus and among the cold and silent mountains, with their ever-present caps of snow, were fresh upon me; and the simple comforts of this quiet American home seemed to beckon me to another home—a home far off in the States, where friends and loved ones doubtless longed for a glimpse of this prodigal. Even as the prodigal on this night longed for a glimpse of them.

On the stage road from Oruro to La Paz, the peak of Kimsa Misa[13] towers within the perennial snow line. Large deposits of tin had recently been discovered there, and rumors of claim jumping were rife. It was ev-ident that the eyes and wits of the prospectors were being sharpened for the struggle to capture a major share of the wealth hidden in those cold, forbidding heights. The stage line had relay posts every twelve or fifteen miles, making signs of human habitation more numerous than on any part of our journey since entering Bolivia. We passed a number of little tented cities, camps of railway engineers, and went through the Indian towns of Velavela and Secaseca before coming in sight of Viscachani,[14] the adobe camp of the railway construction company. Upon our arrival, an invitation to rest a few days required no persuasion. The presence of an excellent American cook, the atmosphere of American hustle and the sounds of American voices were irresistible. While mounted and making a gradual ascent, we had scarcely felt the effect of the high altitude, but in moving about the camp on foot, we suffered shortness of breath for a few days before gradually adjusting to the altitude.

All the grading of the railroad bed between Oruro and La Paz was under subcontract, except two miles of heavy cutting at this camp. The Bolivian government was rendering practical aid by forcing each male Indian to work a week for a reasonable wage. However, this compulsory service was very unsatisfactory, as the Indians had received no training in this class of work. Also, when the week of enforced labor was ended, they could not be induced to continue, not even for greatly increased compensation. As a result, a new crew had to be broken in at the beginning of each week, and progress was anything but satisfactory to the impatient contractors. Ten minutes were allowed the Indians during the forenoon and afternoon, "coca time." During the brief recess, they would chew coca leaves, which have a wonderfully invigorating effect. When almost exhausted, I have stopped for a few minutes, masticated a few of these leaves and then gone forward greatly relieved.[15]

The railway company has years of building before the lines connecting with the cities of Potosi, Cochabamba and Tupiza will be complete. Linking Tupiza with the plateau seems a superhuman undertaking, but the Arroya Railway from Lima to Cerro de Pasco, operating at an altitude of more than 14,000 feet, is evidence of what skilled modern engineering can accomplish. The task taken up by those bold spirits is not a hopeless one.

A few days after our arrival in Viscachani, the general manager visited the camp. He intended to go as far as Oruro by stage and allowed me to ride his horse to Viacha, a railway point of connection with La Paz. Leaving in the afternoon, I halted for the night at a camp thirty miles distant, then proceeded more leisurely the following day, reaching Viacha in time for midday breakfast.

The snowcapped crest of Illimani, more than 21,000 feet above sea level, marks the valley in which La Paz is situated in plain view of El Alto, the terminus of the railroad from Guaqui.[16] From the El Alto station, a forty-minute ride by electric car down a winding railway brought passengers to the eastern suburbs of La Paz, more than a thousand feet below. La Paz, the headquarters of important mining and railway operations, was a scene of great animation. The foreigners devoting their energies to the development of the country's mineral resources were regarded as so many geese engaged in laying golden eggs, and they were being squeezed to the limit by the natives. The hotels were crowded to the doors, and the energies of the proprietors were directed to relieving the guests of as much money as possible rather than to providing the comforts of life. When the day's work was done and dinner, the principal meal of the day, was taken, it was either go to bed or shiver in the hotel buffet, as fires for heating purposes were an unknown luxury, despite the piercing cold. Four woolen blankets failed to keep my numb limbs warm throughout the bitter night.

PART TWO

La Paz to Cumaria

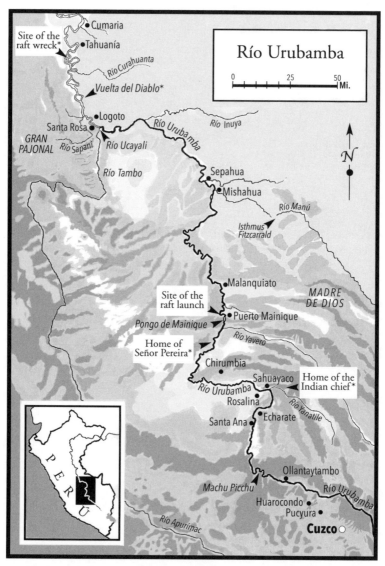

Cumaria
Site of the
raft wreck* Tahuanía
Río Curahuanta

Río Urubamba

0   25   50
|—|—|—|—|—|—|—|—|Mi.

Vuelta del Diablo*

Logoto
Santa Rosa
Río Urubamba   Río Inuya
GRAN
PAJONAL   Río Sapaní   Río Ucayali

Río Tambo   Sepahua

Mishahua

Río Manú

Isthmus
Fitzcarrald

Malanquiato   MADRE
DE DIOS

Site of the
raft launch   Puerto Mainique
Pongo de Mainique
Río Yavero

Home of
Señor Pereira*

Chirumbia

Sahuayaco   Home of the
Indian chief*
Río Urubamba
Rosalina   Río Yanatile

Santa Ana   Echarate

Ollantaytambo

Machu Picchu   Río Urubamba

Huarocondo
Pucyura
Río Apurímac
Cuzco

P E R Ú

*The Urubamba flows northwesterly from southeast of Cuzco to just below
Santa Rosa (present-day Atalaya), where it converges with the Tambo to
form the upper Ucayali. Due to the river's wildly meandering course, the
distance traveled by raft or canoe can be two or three times the distance
in a direct line. Asterisks indicate approximate locations.*

4

⌁

EALEY AND ROY had reached their destination, with no desire to brave the Peruvian jungles toward which our steps had been bent. A chance acquaintance in La Paz—James Orton of Manchester, England—then became my sole companion in the venture to descend the Amazon from its beginning. An experienced victim of the wanderlust himself, he impressed me at once with his sterling worth as a red-blooded man. Orton and I left Mealey and Roy in La Paz and often, oh, how often, we would wish ourselves back in that cheerless city while enduring the hardships and privations that lay before us.

Sailing 12,500 feet above sea level is an experience ordinarily associated with aerial navigation, but it is one that can be enjoyed upon Lake Titicaca,[1] across which our journey led. Occasionally storms sweep the surface of this lake with such violence that the navigators of the modern twin-screw vessels, as well as the Indians in their boats of straw, respect its tempestuous moods. Even in the mildest weather, the shelter of the saloon is agreeable during the night run of 134 miles between Guaqui in Bolivia and Puno in Perú.[2] The practice of allowing the deck passengers to sleep in the after-hold and use the canvas mail pouches stored there for pillows seemed a tribute to the honesty of this class of travelers.

Leaving Orton at Juliaca Junction,[3] I traveled by rail to Arequipa City[4] to purchase the necessities for an expedition from the headwaters of the Amazon. A continuous upgrade climb of 117 miles to an elevation of 14,666 feet, then a tortuous downward rush of 103 miles through a rocky, desolate stretch of jutting hilltops—at places the track reversing and almost overlapping—took me to Arequipa City. This typical Spanish new-world city, with its never-silent church bells and miserably paved streets, is situated in a perennially delightful climate at an altitude of about 7,500 feet. Fortunately, I was domiciled with an Italian-American, who had been in the stampede for gold in California in the days of '49, and enjoyed the pleasure of eating American meals in American fashion—an almost forgotten pleasure. The fame of this caterer has spread throughout western South America, and it is also known that the dyspeptic never gains a second admission to his hospitality, for inability to properly appreciate the delicious creations of his chef exiles the unfortunate for all time. (I might add in passing that a warm welcome waits for me there.) The purchase of arms, ammunition and other equipment completed, the dusty, spirit-exhausting climb to the summit by the tri-weekly train was begun and continued for twelve hours until Juliaca Junction was reached. There Orton was waiting.

We arrived at Sicuani after an all-day journey by rail, first across a gradually rising, almost level expanse, then a drop through a pinching valley flanked by towering peaks, upon whose crests gleamed the cold white of the ever-present snow.[5] Owing to the inaccuracy of the time card, we alighted at a point twenty-five miles from the actual terminus of the railroad. Whether the construction gang outstripped the information of the compilers of the route card or the preparation of the latter was more time-entailing than the building of this section of the road remains a matter of conjecture. The discomfiting fact was that we had no choice but to wait for the next bi-weekly train or walk to the end of the line at Checacupe. We decided to walk.

A stream fed by the eternal snow of the surrounding hills flowed by, rippling against the railroad embankment. As it moves forward, all the while gathering volume and force, it becomes the main headwaters of the Amazon.[6] During the first day's march, this little stream was narrow enough that a nimble person could easily leap across it, but

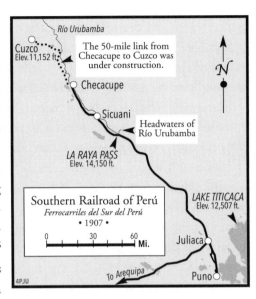

From La Raya Pass northward toward Cuzco, the railway closely followed the Urubamba River. Construction was completed in 1908.

before reaching Checacupe, it increased in volume and depth to such an extent that it had become navigable for light canoes.

When nightfall closed in upon us, we were near an old Spanish house occupied by a family of Inca Indians. Applying for shelter, we were received in a hospitable manner. The house had once been the home of a well-to-do family, and there was about it a melancholy atmosphere of greatness fallen into decay. The main entrance, directly under an imposing watchtower, led into a court, through which a stream of clear water flowed. We were assigned to a suite of two rooms, one containing a massive hardwood settee and cumbersome table, each ornamented with elaborate carving; and the other, a huge four-poster bedstead, so large that an altar in the corner seemed to have been squeezed in place with difficulty.

On the outskirts of Checacupe, the end of our twenty-five-mile walk, collapsing fortifications guard the approach to a rude stone bridge that spans the tributary of the stream we were following. A crumbling sentry box near the end of the bridge and ruins of the temple of the sun worshipers on the summit of the mountain across the main stream were mute evidence of the Inca dynasty.[7]

Along the route by rail from Sicuani to Checacupe, a well-worn trail used by pack trains runs parallel, but from Checacupe to Cuzco, there is a fairly well-kept highway sufficiently wide and level for the operation of a stage line. Mr. Morgan, the English manager of this line, informed us that the next coach would not leave for several days, but added that we could have our baggage conveyed to Cuzco by the traction train[8] leaving in the afternoon. "You may also go on this train, if you wish," he continued, "but if you are in a hurry, you will make better time by walking."

Disregarding Morgan's advice, we took passage on the traction train and were soon in a humor to wonder at his conservatism in reference to the rival systems of transportation. In all my travels, I have never encountered such an instrument of torture. It traveled along at a snail's pace, bouncing up and down in a most distressing manner. When we could endure it no longer, we sprang to the ground and walked ahead. As we became weary of tramping along the rough roadbed, we would sit down and await the coming of the train. Its approach would be announced by the bumping of the wheels, the rattle of loose joints and the locomotive's asthmatic wheezing. Halts were frequent and prolonged. On one occasion, when we had walked ahead and stopped to await it, the train was delayed so long that we finally turned back to investigate. When we reached the train, it seemed intact, but not one of the crew was in sight. A hilarious uproar in a nearby Indian hut suggested a clue, and we discovered the train-men engaged in the ever—to them—irresistible pastime of drinking *chicha*. The engineer, when questioned, said, "We must stop until mañana." How long this meant we could only guess and then hope for deliverance. We had made no provision for an indefinite journey or for prolonged stops to await mañana and were in no humor to enjoy the hilarity afforded by a *chicha* dispensary. However, there was nothing to do but wait. After a time, the engineer, who had reached an advanced stage of conviviality, came out and began drawing the fire from the boiler. When acquainted with the fact that we were hungry, he very considerately, through the persuasive use of the Quechua dialect, induced an Indian in a hut some distance from the scene to provide us with a dish of vegetable stew and a few ears of green corn.

After five days of alternate walking and riding, the latter by far the more painful process of the two, we came within sight of ancient Cuzco, once a capital city of the Incas.[9] Preparations were in full swing for the celebration of what is to these people the most important of all fiestas, that of Corpus Christi. The plaza presented a brilliant appearance, a profusion of gay streamers fluttered from many poles, and a bandstand alive with brilliant combinations of colors occupied the central position.

The morning of the fiesta* witnessed the presence of an almost impenetrable throng of Quechua Indians, swarming in from far and near, every delegation bearing aloft life-sized images that played a prominent part in the subsequent ceremonies. They blocked the narrow streets, a restless, churning mass, each unit attempting to reach a preferred position from which to view the parade. The curb was monopolized by vendors of *chicha* and soggy sweets, and their wares were eagerly bought and as eagerly consumed. The procession, the chief attraction of the day, was headed by government officials, dignitaries of the church and prominent citizens, followed by a vast and motley crowd of Indians. Many of the latter bore the huge images, while others made noises with crude instruments, chiefly drums and whistles. After marching through the streets, the procession entered the cathedral and engaged in the usual religious ceremonies connected with this feast day.[10]

*May 30, 1907

The Indians who did not take part in the parade or religious exercises devoted themselves to the joy of unrestrained indulgence in whatever form of pleasure suggested itself. The varicolored decorations and the gala attire of the people provided a spectacular effect that induced emotional dissipation. Every occasion that offers relaxation from toil—the greatest of all crosses to the Indian—is entered into with much spirit. In fact, one of the greatest obstacles encountered by foreigners engaged in pushing industrial enterprises in this part of the world is the devotion of these people to the fiesta. Holidays are almost innumerable, and on the slightest pretext the people will turn out en masse, forgetting everything except the joy of the moment. As business was at a standstill during this celebration, we had to wait until its effects had worn off before we could make preparations for proceeding to Santa Ana, that outpost town where civilization pauses, backed by the great unknown forest that we were soon to enter.

Tradition says that at the time of the Spanish invasion a graded highway connected Cuzco with Quito, Ecuador. At the present time, Cuzco is the center of the sluggish commercial enterprises of the surrounding countryside and the distribution point for exports from the Santa Ana Valley—coca leaves, chocolate and sugar. Our attempts to purchase two burros for pack animals met with sore disappointment. One party to whom we were referred offered the burros at three times their market value and would not make the slightest reduction. We refused to be "done," but were in a sore predicament until our innkeeper, a Spaniard, came to the rescue by offering to take charge of our dunnage and forward it to Santa Ana by pack train. This suggestion was gladly adopted.

The local market failed to supply several of our needs, chief among them: tobacco. It was practically impossible to get any of the weed, the excessive revenue imposed practically prohibiting its sale, except in the form of rank cigarettes. On the morning of our departure, we had taken leave of our host and gone two blocks when he hurriedly overtook us and explained in an almost inaudible whisper that he had procured some pipe tobacco. We promptly about-faced, and our delight could scarcely find expression when the Spaniard presented us with two pounds of good tobacco. He refused to accept payment and volunteered no information as to where he obtained it. We were cautioned not to expose it to public view since even in Cuzco the inspector in plain clothes is not unknown.

Leaving Cuzco, we paused to inspect an English mission, which seemed in the last throes of a troubled existence. Connected with the mission was a wood- and iron-working establishment that would doubtless have proven a success as a purely industrial enterprise. However, business and Protestant religion form a combination that offers little appeal to the natives of this part of the world. Having partaken freely of the water at Cuzco, we were somewhat jarred when, upon mounting a hill on the outskirts of the city, we observed a number of women washing clothes in the stream from which the water supply was secured. At the moment an epidemic of typhoid fever was raging in the city, and here, no doubt, was the seat of the trouble.

About a mile distant, where an ancient stone fortification spanned the road, a summit afforded a splendid view of the surrounding countryside.[11] From this point the pack train descended at times very sharply, the drop from the quaint Indian city of Cuzco to Santa Ana being from 11,100 to 3,500 feet above sea level. The first day out, having separated from the pack train, we were on foot and made fifteen miles before halting for the night at Pucyura.[12] Our arrival there excited the curiosity of the local government official, his family and friends to an unusual degree, and all of them gathered about us in the evening to ask about our nationality, where we came from, where we were going, what we were going for and such other questions as suggested themselves.

Our route on the following day led through the Indian town

of Huarocondo,[13] and about midday we came again upon the river. Following its course through a canyon until nightfall, we halted at an Indian hut and, by means of signs to the head of the house, expressed our desire to spend the night. As he seemed dull of comprehension, we produced a piece of cheap jewelry, and thereupon the scales dropped from his eyes. We were motioned into the hut and our host acted from that moment as if our coming were an event he had looked forward to with great longing. The most conspicuous thing in the Indian huts we encountered along this route were huge native copper kettles used chiefly for brewing *chicha*, the universal drink. Every hut contained one or more of these.

About forty miles from Cuzco, approached through a pinching valley with barriers of such height that the sun does not reach the river level until midday, we saw overtopping terraces on each side of the stream. These terraces constituted the outlying fortifications of Olliante Fort.[14] A short distance further and the fort proper was encountered. This fortress, though built hundreds of years ago, has withstood the ravages of time so well that to the casual observer it seems as impregnable as when its grim walls were first erected. Most remarkable was the state of the cement used in the construction of the pile, for after so many years of exposure, it showed no evidence of crumbling. Stone steps led from the first floor to the upper tiers, so narrow that it was impossible to walk two abreast. Innumerable spiders and other insects now inhabit these passages, and grass grows on terraced floors that resounded to the cry of battle in the militant days of long ago. Tradition says that the fortification was built to prevent the abduction of the Inca princess. Thus, even in this wild and remote country, one is reminded that woman has always been a potent factor in the making of history.

Beyond Olliante Tambo, where we spent the night, we entered the forest line, and trees of various sizes and descriptions were seen, furnishing a grateful change to eyes grown weary of barren walls and bald projections. The Santa Ana Valley begins at this point, Olliante Fort marking the approach to a gradually widening area of cultivated land. Through this valley, every farm is irrigated from a mountain stream tapped at a point sufficiently elevated to ensure distribution. Sugarcane, from which a very strong rum is distilled and for the manufacture of which every farm has its own still, is grown in considerable quantities, but the greater part of the irrigated land is planted in coca trees, the leaves of which enter very largely into the life of the Indian. Reference has been made to the remarkable sustaining power of the juice of these leaves, and their virtue is well known to the Indians there. During his daily labor, the Indian has fixed periods for consuming coca leaves, and he never starts on a journey without a bag containing a quantity sufficient to meet his requirements until his return. When traveling—always on foot—the Indian halts about every two hours, thoroughly masticates a few of the leaves, swallows the juice and pulp, to which a minute pinch of alkali[15] has been added, and then resumes the journey. Fifty miles is regarded as only an ordinary journey for one day.

The opinion prevails among denizens of this valley that it is an admission of inferiority for one to sleep out of doors at night. One day, after an extraordinarily long walk, we pitched our camp beneath a great overhanging rock, near which a brook wended its way toward the river. The chill of the higher altitude was about us, but the surrounding timber furnished ample fuel for a good campfire—rarest of all luxuries—and soon we were enjoying life to the fullest extent. About this time an Indian approached and informed us that we could find shelter at a nearby house. When we told him we preferred to remain where we were, he seemed utterly confounded. He did not realize that as we sat about the campfire, puffing our pipes, we were enjoying one of the most delightful experiences of many days. The Andean Indian will not sit near a fire. There is a widespread superstition that fire causes rheumatism. and these people, when sleeping in a camp where a fire is blazing, place their blankets entirely out of the range of its glow.

The last night en route to Santa Ana was spent at the home of a retired Peruvian army officer who operated quite an extensive farm. He had just received a Pelton wheel[16] for developing power on a mountain stream, and when he learned that we could advise him where and how this wheel could be placed to best advantage, it was with great difficulty that we escaped his hospitality. It was our intention to press forward early the following day, but our host was so urgent in his requests that we did not get away until late in the afternoon. We remained and assisted him, our departure taken in the face of vehement requests to prolong our stay.

Three miles from this farm, after ascending a steep hill, Santa Ana[17] burst upon our view, a quaintly primitive town occupying a spreading area at the junction of a stream flowing from the west and Río Santa Ana,[18] the stream we were following. At nightfall we entered this town, the center of a great, silent valley where scarcely an echo of the busy outer world seems to penetrate, a valley that appears to have borrowed from the mist and mystery of the forest beyond its borders, where the slumber of the ages remains unbroken.

An Indian led us to the home of Señor Villafuerte, to whom we bore a letter of introduction and into whose care our baggage had been consigned. "Enter; my house is your home" was his cordial greeting. After dinner the local padre and Señor Duque,[19] a prominent citizen of the village, impelled by hospitality and perhaps a bit of pardonable curiosity, called upon our host. The introduction of Señor Duque was followed by the question: "Surely you are Frenchmen?"

"No, an American and an Englishman," I replied.

He wanted to know more about our journey, expressed his willingness to assist in every way possible when we were ready to proceed and invited us to spend some of our stay with him. Señor Duque was one of three brothers of Austrian descent. He was the manager of the

Santa Ana farm jointly owned by the brothers, while the others gave their attention to a mutual enterprise in another part of Perú. At the home of this very excellent host, we noticed a piano in the sitting room where we were enjoying a smoke after dinner. This instrument had been brought from Cuzco on the shoulders of Indians, twenty powerful brown-skins performing the remarkable feat in ten days' time. Señor Duque informed us that Señor Tell of the Sahuayaco farm had but recently returned from a trip into the interior and would be in a position to advise us. We were further furnished with a cordial letter of introduction, and after two days spent very pleasantly at Santa Ana, we took our departure, having in the meantime secured a horse and an Indian attendant to convey our baggage.

Crossing Río Santa Ana, we ascended an outreaching spur of the valley barriers and at its summit, paused to view the surrounding valley, the home of a privileged few who lived in indolent care through a system of semi-slavery that prevails both in Bolivia and Perú. Under the law, the peón class[20] is bound to render service for debt contracted with the patrón class. One patrón can transfer the service of an indebted peón to another patrón for a consideration; if the peón deserts, he can be brought back by force and compelled to discharge the debt. As each plantation is provided with a distillery, the weakness of the Indian for drink is encouraged in a measure, and the great majority are kept in increasing servitude. Thus, drink, which enslaves in theory in some lands, enslaves in fact in this country. Sunday is the day almost universally given over to drinking, while Monday is "sober-up day." Only five work days in a week are required of the peón, the extra day being allowed for him to recover from the excessive indulgences of the Sabbath.

After a journey of twenty miles, we entered a cultivated expanse of sugarcane and coca bushes, and then were upon the Echarate estate, one of the largest and most productive plantations in the valley.[21] The residence of the proprietor, flanked by the modest quarters of the peóns, was most imposing. It called to mind the old days below Mason's and Dixon's line, when the "big house" surrounded by the cabins of the black slaves, was the most conspicuous feature of life down South. The servants here were respectful and active, their conduct reminding one of the faithful devotion of those of the antebellum South.[22]

When acquainted with our purpose to invade the wilderness, Señor Polo, our host, cautioned us concerning the difficulties of the journey and considerately offered us a letter to the chief of the rubber camp[23] at Mainique, toward which our route led. Our conversation with Señor Polo followed an elaborate meal that proved highly enjoyable after the hard tramp of the day. Dining with these people is an art, and dinner is the social event of the day. The element of time does not enter it at all, the meal being brought to a conclusion only when the laughter and chatter seems to have run its course.

In passing through this valley, everyone we met displayed the liveliest curiosity as to our destination, nationality and intentions. As a result of this frequent examination, we were delayed considerably in going from Echarate to Sahuayaco,[24] almost twice the necessary time for the journey. Upon our arrival at Sahuayaco, we found Señor Tell, to whom we carried a letter of introduction, confined to his home by ill health. He had penetrated the forest of the Yavero district,[25] lost his bearings, wandered around for a week or ten days before finding his way, was without means of making a fire, had slept in wet clothing and was then suffering from rheumatism and fever, the result of such exposure.

He invited us to remain at his place for several days while arrangements were made for us to go by canoe to the Pongo Rapids. After halting for two days, the prospect of proceeding by canoe seemed favorable, judging from information received from Rosalina,[26] a point twenty-five miles distant along our route, and we set out for that place, expecting to find the canoes there. A few miles from Sahuayaco, shortly after entering a thick forest, we came upon a Quechua Indian and a forest savage* preparing a meal at the foot of a trail that led over the mountains to the Río Yanatile crossing.[27] The Quechua spoke broken Spanish, and after much linguistic effort, we learned that he and the savage were from the rubber camp of Lombardi & Co. and were en route to Echarate for a supply of medicine. After a short halt, we resumed our journey, climbing the mountain trail only by great exertion. After descent by a tortuous footpath to Río Yanatile, a swift stream issuing from the hills, we crossed just above its confluence with the Santa Ana and proceeded until we came to the main stream, now called Río Urubamba.

Following the river at nightfall, we were short of our destination, so we accepted the hospitality of Miguel, who lived on the river near the trail. A brother of the paramount chief of this district, he was waited upon and pampered by the numerous women connected with his home, and devoted most of his time to hunting and fishing. He seemed to take much pride in his position as well as in his well-kept household, but the object about which his affections seemed to center most largely was a cheap sixteen-bore, breach-loading shotgun. We were unable to learn where or how he obtained this weapon, but it was evidently the apple of his eye, and the fact that he did not have any ammunition with which to make it bark and bring down game did not make him less solicitous about it. He had yards of greasy cloth wrapped about it, and while unwinding the mass in order to display his treasure, he repeatedly declared that it was the most wonderful thing in all the land. After he had displayed the weapon and pointed out all its marvelous aspects, we displayed our arms—a sixteen-bore repeating shotgun and a heavy-caliber repeating rifle—and when his eyes fell upon them, he became an example of ecstatic admiration.

*Throughout Williams's narrative, the noun *savage* should be understood to mean "a person belonging to a primitive society," not a tribesman who practiced cruelty or violence.

He had been greatly interested in my six-shooter, but when he saw the repeating shotgun, his desire to possess it became almost over-whelming. A present of a few rounds of ammunition for his gun was not sufficient to take the keen edge off his disappointment when he learned that he could not gain possession of the more modern weapon.

Disappointment was in store for us in the matter of the canoe. The man who was to carry us to the Pongo Rapids by this means of transportation said that unforeseen hindrances compelled him to postpone his departure for two months at least. He revived our hopes, however, by saying that the paramount chief was making preparations to dispatch two canoes in a few days. It was decided thereupon that I should interview the chief while Orton returned to Sahuayaco.

After a zigzag climb of six miles at an elevation of 5,000 feet above the river level, I arrived at the settlement of Chief Pedro, who at one time was the supreme chief of all the surrounding country, having dominion over the savages as well as the Quechua Indians. However, his influence over the savages was about at an end, as he had neglected them and had lived more as an Inca, of which race he was a surviving chief. In his old age, mastered by inherent inclinations, he had made his home upon the summit of the highest accessible mountain and had thereby cut himself off from the savages whose home is ever in the depth of the wilderness.

Upon greeting Chief Pedro, I was invited into a room in one of the detached buildings, and there food was provided. After a brief rest, I was again invited into the presence of the chief, who inquired in fluent Castilian[28] concerning our adventure.

"The interior," he said with a solemn shake of his head, "is full of bewildering danger and to venture on the river beyond the rapids is extremely perilous."

"We are fixed on our determination to go," I replied.

"Very well," he said with a solemn shake of his head. "If you insist upon going, you may travel in my canoes as far as the Pongo Rapids.[29] In the meantime, make my house your home. I have coffee, chocolate and milk, and will have a beef slaughtered." Then he repeated, "Make my house your home."

This gracious greeting and invitation sounded fine, but that very night a messenger from the agent of Lombardi & Co., the owners of the Pongo de Mainique rubber concession, arrived bringing a present of twenty gallons of rum. This gift from the enterprising agent destroyed our last hope of getting to the interior by canoe. For three hilarious days, I endured the hospitality of Chief Pedro and then departed. During these days, not a soul on the place was allowed to sleep. It was just one grand hurrah from dusk to dawn with no prospect of letup until the last drop of rum had disappeared down the throat of his majesty or those of his thrice-willing subjects. Before leaving, I took the precaution to thank the son of the chief for the hospitality shown me by his father and, finally escaping his affectionate embrace, made hasty tracks for Sahuayaco to confer anew with Orton and Señor Tell, who insisted upon our remaining with him until further developments. As there seemed nothing else to do, the invitation was accepted.

Señor Tell resided with a family of Argentine and American descent. Many years earlier, Señor Don Luis Gonzales[30] emigrated from Argentina to this valley, where he met and wed the daughter of a native of Maryland who had married and brought up a family there. Señora Gonzales was keenly interested in that far wonderland, the home of her dead father, and never tired of asking questions concerning it.

After a wait of several days, definite information was received that the canoe voyage was hopeless, so other arrangements had to be made if the trip into the interior was to be continued. We had no intention of turning back, having come this far. Learning that two Indians we met on our journey to Rosalina would return by land in a few days to the rubber camp below the Pongo Rapids, we determined to go with them if possible. Señor Tell sent for a Quechua who, after much argument as to terms, agreed to carry a part of our dunnage and act as a guide. But he said it would be necessary for him to wait until the arrival of certain communications that were to come from Cuzco for transmission by him to the rubber camp. The date upon which these communications would arrive was as uncertain as the span of human life. It might be today, tomorrow, next week or next month; no one knew. Moreover, no one except my companion and I was concerned about it. If it is true that time is money, then these people are rich beyond the dreams of avarice. A day to them is as a week, and a week is as a day. The rising of today's sun is nothing, nor yet its going down. Other suns will rise as fair and sink with equal splendor. So, in the philosophy of this people, there is no occasion to worry over a few days or a few weeks of delay.

Orton proceeded to Rosalina with the Indian guide while I remained with Señor Tell, awaiting the communications that were to mark the resumption of our journey and also studying the character and habits of the Quechua people. Their home life is quiet, peaceful and happy. There is none of the vain striving after social position that so often injects discord into the lives of the socially inclined in the modern cities of the world. The gulf between the peón and the patrón is as fixed as that which the scriptural writer describes as standing between Abraham and the rich man whose dogs licked the sores of Lazarus.[31] The middle class—the terror and despair of the upper crust in the United States—is unknown here, which may be due in large measure to the atmosphere of peace that envelops the country. The strenuous spirit inseparably associated with the middle classes of more advanced countries is conspicuous by its absence, and not even an echo of the noise the ambitious ones make in the great world struggle for place penetrates this valley.

After dinner, the evening was spent in languid rest beneath the tropical trees in the garden, where the incense of flowers walks like a presence when the cool winds whisper. Conversation, quite spirited as the evening meal progressed, now relaxes under the subduing influence of the gathering night. As the stars swing into place beaming with dazzling beauty and brilliancy, and the caressing tones of the soft guitar light out upon the night from the portico above where the ladies are assembled, silence and a great peace steal over all.

The local padre, who was on an itinerant round at this time, proved himself an excellent entertainer. One evening during a lull in the conversation, he asked, "You have visited Buenos Aires?"

"Yes, padre," I replied.

"And are acquainted with the neighborhood of Calle Defensa?"

"Quite well."

"Very good," he said, continuing, "At the corner of Defensa and Belgrano there stands an old cathedral that is associated with the early history of the city. The tower still bears scars left by the English invasion of nearly a hundred years ago. Within the walls of this temple of worship is preserved a flag captured during that unsuccessful effort of the British to widen their domain. Many years later, at a time when the Argentine had awakened to a lively appreciation of a second English invasion—that of British capital—the government magnanimously offered to return this historic memento of a losing fight to Great Britain. When the offer was received, it was rejected with a curt statement that when the flag was wanted, England would come and take it. Of course I cannot vouch for this story, but certain it is that the flag still molders in the old cathedral where it was placed generations ago."[32]

"Padre, you have heard the anecdote of the Yankee skipper and the wooden nutmeg?" inquired Señor Tell.

The question was followed by a negative reply, and then Señor Tell repeated the old story of Yankee thrift—and Yankee trickery—that has belted the earth.[33]

This yarn reminded the padre of a German skipper who unloaded a lot of sardines upon the unsuspecting citizens of Iquitos, the discovery being made following his departure that the sardines were manufactured of paper and oil. That Yankee skipper was vindicated on the score that "there are others."

The second week of my sojourn with Señor Tell witnessed active preparations for the marriage of three doting pairs of Quechua Indians. A fiesta lasting two days was the first conspicuous preliminary to this interesting triple ceremony. During this period, the Indians drank and feasted to their utmost capacity, and all thought of work was forgotten. Upon the arrival of the fateful hour when the bonds were to be welded, the six Indians, each with expressionless face, stood before the padre and the ceremony was performed. While the fiesta preceding the marriage ceremony is one of unrestricted gaiety, the ceremony itself is a deeply solemn affair, and the assembled guests looked more as if they are witnessing the last sad rites above the grave of a fellow rather than the happy consummation of a tender romance. Three events stand out strongly in the lives of these people, and their importance is not overshadowed by any other: the birth of a child, the marriage of a couple and the death of one of their number.

Nothing else in life seems of much importance. Yet, despite the solemnity with which the Indians enter into marriage relations, the vows are worn but lightly and desertions are of frequent occurrence. The triple marriage was followed by ten days of celebration, the principal amusements being dancing, singing and feasting. The dance resembles the Spanish fandango and was accompanied by the beating of tom-toms, weird chanting and monotonous handclapping. The servitude of these Indians is in striking contrast to the station they occupied prior to the Spanish invasion. In the days of the Inca dynasty, they represented the highest type of Western civilization. Today, they are a degenerate race held in a condition of semi-slavery, owing in part to their love of the flowing bowl.

5

⌃⌃⌃

WE WAITED seventeen days before a native runner brought news that the long-expected communication had arrived from Cuzco and that the Quechua and forest savage would pass en route to the Pongo. Upon receiving this information, Señor Gonzales provided an Indian guide to accompany me as far as Rosalina. Despite my anxiety to join Orton there, it was with a feeling of genuine regret that I left these kind benefactors. They urged me to write should we ever succeed in getting through the great wilderness inscribed upon the Peruvian maps as "unexplored" and "unknown."

En route to Rosalina, while ascending the mountain between Sahuayaco and Río Yanatile, I saw a red deer,[1] and in stalking it with more eagerness than caution, lost the trail and my Indian guide. But I could see the bare summit of the mountain towards which our course lay and judged that it would be possible to work my way around it. Presently I was confronted with an almost impossible descent, but it seemed the only way, and I attempted it. Sliding down the deep incline from bush to bush, I made fairly safe progress until suddenly one of the bushes eluded my grasp, and I tobogganed along at an alarming rate for a distance of about fifty feet, accompanied by an avalanche of small stones. My descent ended in a sheer drop of about ten feet over a cliff. That I escaped serious injury was marvelous. When the vicinity of the river was finally reached, I found it necessary to cut my way to the edge of a stream, the undergrowth being so rank and thick. But I succeeded in swimming across and a short distance beyond found the trail that led to the main river.[2] A shot finally brought the Indian, and we proceeded. The net result of this mishap was a delay of half a day and a number of painful bruises.

Miguel, the chief's brother who will be recalled as a great admirer of our repeating shotgun, insisted that I remain a day with him when I reached his place, and the invitation was accepted. He arranged a wild hog hunt the following morning, but our tramp into the forest was unsuccessful. While we were resting by the hut later in the day, one of his retainers rushed up with the information that an animal had been treed near the river. I offered my weapon to Miguel, feeling sure that he would be delighted to try his skill, and his first shot he brought down the game. This animal, though weighing only about fifty pounds, bore a striking resemblance to a bear,[3] and its flesh proved very palatable. It was prepared at once, and, though there were only six men in the party, every vestige of it had been consumed by the following morning.

Early the next day I rejoined Orton at Rosalina and explained that if we continued the trip we would have to carry packs weighing more than fifty pounds each for a distance of about 150 miles and depend upon our guns for food.

"I am for going on" was his reply. "I think we can get through in about ten days."

Brave, splendid fellow, Orton. Danger never caused him dismay, nor peril a desire to turn back. We determined to start the following morning and at once began assorting our belongings, as it was necessary to abandon everything that was not absolutely needed.

With the exception of the forest savage we had encountered near Sahuayaco, this race was entirely new to us, and it was with great interest that we saw a number of them for the first time, dressed in native costumes and adorned with tribal markings. The costumes of the men consisted of a single garment, made much like a sack and dyed a dull red. To obtain any reliable information of the interior was practically impossible. The Quechua and his patrón are on a common level when it comes to any knowledge of the interior. A journey of a few days is regarded as a most momentous event, and months are spent in preparing for it. We announced our intention of each packing fifty pounds into that forbidding territory and were regarded with amazement: "White men seldom walk and never bear burdens."

On the morning of July 12, 1907, we began the journey into the interior, accompanied only by Alacon the Quechua and the savage. The trail led to the summit of a mountain about 4,000 feet above the river level. The Indians, though burdened with their own packs weighing about a hundred pounds each, made the ascent with apparent ease, but that climb called for the utmost strength of Orton and myself. At times it seemed we had reached the limit of our endurance, but we pushed on, taking brief rests occasionally and encouraging one another with cheering words.

We reached the summit of the mountain in about three hours, and in a northerly direction from its peak we beheld a magnificent expanse of forest. Looking backward about three miles distant we could see the home of Chief Pedro, paramount chief of all that region, who had promised so much before the arrival of the rum from the agent of the rubber company. To the right, overlooking Río Chirumbia, was a settlement of Dominican friars—the last connecting link with civilization.

A sharp descent brought us to Río Chirumbia, a small, clear stream flowing from the east. The Indians plunged into the water and waded across without hesitation, the Quechua indifferent to the soaking his trousers received and the savage not taking the trouble to lift his garments. We paused long enough to remove shoes and trousers before wading, much to the disgust of our guide, Alacon, exclaiming, "Hurry, señores, we are losing much time." The icy temperature of the water was refreshing after the hard climb and hasty descent, and we treated the request to hurry with an indifference that must have seemed unreasonable. Prior to leaving, time had been to them the most inconsequential thing on earth, so it was strange that they should suddenly become obsessed with the idea that we should hasten each shining moment.

Having resumed the march after this short delay we made fair progress until about noon and then halted to prepare tea. Beyond Río Chirumbia the trail was easier and certainly more picturesque. It led along the face of a towering cliff overhanging Río Chano, a small stream that wound through the valley hundreds of feet below. About four o'clock, after a tramp of about eighteen miles, Alacon informed us that it would be impossible to reach the next stream before dark, and we halted for the night. We were almost ready to drop in our tracks, and it was with infinite relief that we laid our packs aside and made preparations for supper. After the meal we lighted our pipes and were at ease. From overhead we heard the harsh cry of the long-tailed parrots, whose varicolored bodies flashed in the light of the declining day. It seemed I had scarcely fallen asleep when I was aroused by the cry of these birds as they started for the feeding grounds upon the dawn of the new day. My half-smoked pipe lay beside me, where it had fallen when sleep overtook me. Stiff limbs and sore shoulders were grim reminders of the hard journey of the preceding day.

"Do you feel sore?" I asked Orton.

"Don't ask fool questions," he answered, sufficiently clear to one who could appreciate how he felt.

Breakfast of tea and yuca root gruel[4] was taken in the gray mist of the early morning, and before the sun began to trace its colors upon the eastern horizon, we were ready to resume our journey. Alacon at this point offered to relieve us of half the weight of our packs, saying he and the savage would carry the additional weight for one sol.[5] But we had engaged them to act as guides and carry as much of the outfit as they could march under. Our load was reduced accordingly, and the Indians moved forward under the additional load—without the sols or apparent effort.

Our course from the camp followed a northerly direction, at times worming around high cliffs, as if to afford us a view of the apparently endless expanse of forest into which we were plunging. Parrots screamed overhead, and on two occasions there was a crash among the undergrowth and droves of wild hogs stampeded across the trail, uttering grunts of defiance as they fled. Occasionally we heard the chatter of monkeys overheard, and this invariably meant a few minutes rest, for the Indians seemed very fond of the meat of these animals. Discarding their packs, they would creep about, uttering a peculiar whistling sound to lure the monkeys within range of our guns. On the second day of our march, one fell victim to this sound, and the Indians enjoyed a feast of roast monkey that night. They were generous to offer us some, but we were satisfied to make our meal of yuca gruel and a small quail-like bird Orton had killed earlier.

That day Alacon complained that the packs were too heavy and expressed his fear that the savage might desert if not relieved of some of the weight. They had moved along with such speed that Orton and I found it difficult to keep up with them, and we decided this was merely a pretext for demanding more money. At one time, Alacon laid down his pack and refused to shoulder it unless relieved of a part of its contents. When he did this, I produced a special permit issued at Arequipa and, pointing to the official seal, intimated that the Peruvian government was behind us and that the guide would get into trouble if he refused to comply with the terms of his contract. This display of what seemed to be a formidable legal document had the desired effect; he gathered up his pack and resumed the journey.

We marched twenty-eight miles that day and were more than ever persuaded that the Indians were not overloaded

Again that night we were asleep as soon as supper had been disposed of. When morning came, Orton, who was first awake, exclaimed, "The Indians are gone." It was true. Whether they had been frightened away by the official seal in my pocket or had fled as a means of punishing us for not complying with their demands was a matter of speculation. There was, however, nothing speculative about the predicament in which we had been left. Deep in the forest, with all our goods and without a guide, we had been deserted.

The Indians, who had doubtless fled as soon as we went to sleep, took none of our belongings, and this led us to believe that their flight was due in a large measure to the picture of vague but official authority conjured up in the mind of Alacon by the formidable but absolutely harmless permit I had made the mistake of displaying. Alacon enjoyed an unusual amount of freedom, comparatively speaking; he was the master of his goings and comings, having managed to avoid indebtedness through the most extraordinary habit of not drinking. Perhaps my display of authority suggested a curtailment of his privilege.

After calmly discussing the situation, we decided to push on. We had already traveled hundreds of miles and endured many hardships that we might explore the mysteries of this forest. To turn back meant failure, a thing we were not ready to admit. Opening our packs, we went over the contents with great care, laying aside every article that was not necessary to sustain life and protect us from the dangers ahead. We reduced our outfit to less than a hundred pounds weight, and this we divided between us, leaving the remainder to the tender mercies of the forest. Our food supply was two small bottles of salt and about one pound of tea—but of matches, luckily a supply that should last for weeks.

The fleeing guides had doubtless entertained no thought but that we would turn back, and they made no effort to conceal their course. We decided that they would make at once for the rubber camp at Puerto Mainique, with which they were connected, and we started out in pursuit. Misplaced vines, broken twigs and trampled grass made the path clear for a time, and we had no difficulty in following them. Feeling sure that we could reach Río Yavero[6] without trouble, unless attacked by hostile savages, we set out briskly despite the added weight we were forced to carry.

An edible palm was discovered where we halted for lunch at noon. After laborious hacking with machetes, we felled it and cut out the soft growth at the root of the leaves. Eaten raw with a sprinkle of salt, this growth satisfies hunger; when boiled, it makes a most nutritious and palatable soup. A few days after one of these trees is felled, worms gather in the pith, and the savages consider these a great delicacy when fried. In this country ignorance is bliss in matters relating to the culinary arts. On one occasion I was served a tempting dish that I devoured with great relish, only to learn later that grasshoppers were the chief ingredient.

We lunched at the summit of a hill, beyond which the trail led along innumerable reverses with a drop of 300 to 400 feet to the mile. From this elevation, we could trace the course of Río Yavero for many miles toward its source in the Madre de Dios district.[7] In an air line, its nearest turn was not more than five miles, but by the serpent-like trail, the distance was fully eighteen miles. We followed the path left by the Indians without a great deal of trouble, and about four o'clock in the afternoon, I suggested that Orton take it easy while I walked on ahead and pitched our camp for the night at the first water. Not quite as young as myself, he consented, and I put forth rapidly. In a short while I encountered a marshy depression, a swamp covered with rank overgrowth, but, supposing it would soon be left behind, I continued on. Soon I had penetrated so far into this soggy depression that it was impossible to turn back. Owing to the approach of night,

I hastened forward with the greatest possible speed, hoping to find an elevated spot before darkness overtook me. I ran whenever the ground would permit it and reached a strip of high ground just as the last rays of the dying day were fading from the forest depths. It was quite dark by the time a few branches had been collected and a fire started. In the meantime, having heard nothing from Orton and fearing that he had become lost in the swamp, I built the fire up until it burned almost to the treetops and called repeatedly at the top of my voice. Yet not a sound came from the dismal depths of the swamp, save the vibrant cry of some wild beast. There was not a drop of water in the vicinity of the camp, and I was nearly famished.

An hour or more passed, and then, realizing that the chances of Orton joining me before morning were very slender, I gathered an additional supply of wood and spread my blanket on the ground and attempted to find relief in sleep. A moment later I felt an insect crawling upon my neck and, upon investigation, found that I had made my bed near the highway of an army of coque ants.[8] Hundreds of them had penetrated the lining of my coat, and numerous small holes bore witness to the vigor with which they sawed their way into the material. These ants, though not venomous, destroy everything they come in contact with that can be penetrated by their remarkable cutting blades. They travel through the forest in great armies, wearing a path several inches wide, and it was near one of these paths that I had unfortunately made my camp. As a protective measure, I placed my coat and blanket in the dunnage bag and hung the latter upon a limb. Then, gathering up a lot of dry leaves, I distributed them about the camp and set them on fire, hoping to prevent another invasion. I had scarcely finished this when a deep, vicious growl sounded from the underbrush, just at my back. Seizing my machete, I sprang to the fire, heaped on a lot of rubbish and stood waiting, hoping that the flare-up would frighten the animal and cause it to flee. The leap of the flames as they swirled among the branches overhead was followed by silence, but they had no sooner died than a spitting snarl came from the underbrush—again at my back.

The persistence of this animal, which I felt sure was a jaguar,[9] caused me to feel decidedly uncomfortable, and I decided as a further measure of protection to build a second fire and sit between the two. While engaged in this, it was impossible to keep my face towards the animal slinking in the underbrush. It persistently kept behind me. In daylight the suspense would soon have been over, but at night it was different. Every stir in the forest attracted my attention, and as I peered with straining eyes into the dark beyond the circle of the fire-light, the creature seemed to be stealthily moving among the shadows. Again, I fancied I could hear its steps behind me and shuddered as I imagined the animal suddenly leaping from the darkness and sinking its claws into my flesh. I hesitated to fire my gun into the darkness of where the animal might have been, fearing that I should have to deal with a jaguar maddened by a wound as well as by blood lust, but the suspense finally became so great that I could endure it no longer.

The explosion of my heavy-caliber rifle, confined by the thick growth, was like that of a cannon, but there followed the welcome sound of crashing undergrowth as the animal dashed from the scene. The roar awoke the forest. Birds chirped and monkeys chattered in the distance while almost overhead some wild turkeys were heard to gobble. The situation was not so uncomfortable now, but realizing that more wood would be required to keep the fires going until morning, I gingerly ventured around, machete in hand, and collected enough dry branches to last until dawn. In the meantime, my parched throat and cracked lips cried aloud for water, but there was none to be had. A handful of coca leaves allayed my hunger, but intensified the thirst.

At last, thoroughly exhausted, I slept fitfully until the call of a wild turkey brought me bounding to my feet with the thought of breakfast uppermost in my mind. Making my way near the roost, I watched until daylight, for the forest was yet wrapped in the uncertain shadows of early morning. Waiting until the light grew strong enough to see the sights on my rifle, I fired at a turkey that showed dimly against a streak of gray daylight. It fell and as others upon the limb arose with the report, I brought down a second one.

By the time I had broiled the turkeys over the coals and eaten one, it was seven o'clock, yet Orton had not appeared. The tortures of thirst forced me to push on in search of water, but I left a note pinned to an upright stick, explaining to Orton that I would halt at the first stream and directing attention to the second turkey, which I suspended from a limb.

I had proceeded only about 400 yards when I discovered a small red deer drinking from a brook that crept across the trail. Without pausing to dislodge my pack I dropped to one knee and fired. The shock of the heavy bullet caused the deer to drop almost in its tracks, and I hurried forward, my first act upon reaching its side being to fall upon my knees and drink long and deep from the brook. After opening the jugular vein of the deer I went forward to see if a more suitable place for a camp could be found. Luckily one was near at hand, and I was engaged in building a fire when, much to my relief, Orton appeared. He had discovered my note a few minutes after I left it and was engaged in eating the turkey when the report of my gun brought him hurrying along the trail.

While we skinned the deer and prepared to smoke the meat, Orton related his experience during the night. He had started into the swamp upon my heels, but turned back before it was too late and made his camp on the trail at a point where it ran around a sharp cliff. And he, too, had spent a sleepless night. An animal had repeatedly attempted to follow the trail and drew so close at one point, approaching with great stealth, that Orton barely had time to throw a burning limb from the fire into its face before it came within striking distance. The missile had the desired effect, for the animal hastily disappeared, but it left Orton in a state that forbade slumber. We decided then and there that it would not be wise to separate, and from that time forward we tried to sleep within hailing distance at all times.

As the entire day was spent in smoking the deer, both of us attempted to sleep at times, but numerous swarms of flies became so troublesome that sleep was out of the question. With the coming of night, we built three fires and slept within the triangle. The flies, which had made life almost unbearable during the day, disappeared as if by magic, and we slept peacefully, our slumber disturbed only by the reverberant crash of falling trees. At intervals, both day and night, the fall of decayed trees and limbs sent echoes resounding through the forest. We saw more than one great giant of the woods stretch its length upon the earth, there to lie until swallowed up in the dust of decay. Occasionally one of these huge trees would carry down smaller ones, and these in turn cause others to fall, until the forest would resound with the roar and crash. It was as if these inanimate things had taken on life and were engaged in a mighty battle for supremacy.

From this point slow progress was made in following the trail of the Indians as it led through undergrowth that became almost impenetrable at times. The Indians could easily pass through openings that were difficult for us to enter, and we found it necessary to cut our way through many places.

On the afternoon of the second day from the camp where we had halted to smoke the deer, we crossed a small stream and shortly afterwards saw a palm-thatched hut. Our approach was disputed by a disreputable looking dog, whose barking brought an Indian child around a corner of the hut. The moment it caught sight of us, the youngster made a dash for cover, and a moment later an adult Indian appeared. He gazed upon us in silence and with characteristic stolidity as we drew near. He answered our greeting in Machiguenga,[10] but our knowledge of this dialect was so limited that we could not follow him and resorted to sign language. A bright colored handkerchief, with a picture of an animal for a centerpiece, was presented as a peace offering, and we were motioned to a seat under a shelter of palm leaves. After a brief wait, a squaw appeared and placed some boiled fish and yuca root before us. By drawing to the fullness of our knowledge of the Machiguenga tongue, we finally made the Indians understand that we wanted some boiling water. Then we made some tea and offered some to the couple. The head of the house tasted it, with evident disappointment, and put his hand on one of the canteens in a very suggestive manner. We offered him a little bit of the rum, but as we had put some medicinal herbs in it, he drank it with a very wry face. The presence of the herbs no doubt saved us much annoyance. Among all the Indians encountered even in the most inaccessible parts of the Amazon basin, rum was known and appreciated to the fullest extent. A quart of rum would buy more than a hundred times its value in food or services.

As the day following our arrival at the Indian hut was the Sabbath, we made it a day of rest. In the afternoon, I found a deep place in the stream nearby and went in swimming. While enjoying the water, I heard voices on the shore and, looking around, saw a group of men and women congregated and watching me with evident interest. Finally, the curiosity of several became so great that they plunged into the water and approached close enough to touch me. Both men and women put forth their fingers and touched my flesh, after which they looked at the digits as if expecting some of the white to come off. It was plain from their presence that they had never before seen a white man. I made them understand that such familiarity was not appreciated, and they retreated to the shore, jabbering a while as if greatly interested. When they finally withdrew, it was with many ughs and ahs, very likely discussing the white that would not rub off.

That afternoon the Indians who had displayed such a lively

curiosity while I was bathing appeared at the hut and presented us with two brilliantly plumed macaws, birds that are very palatable when young. Inasmuch as the cooking of the squaw had not been to our liking, we determined to prepare these birds ourselves and, having appropriated a pot, were engaged in making a stew when our host made it clear that cooking did not fit into his ideas of what a man should do. Perhaps he saw with prophetic vision what might happen if two white men set such an example in the presence of his squaw. At any rate, he seemed determined that the future should not be bestrewn with disputes as to who should preside at the pot, and he promptly called the squaw, instructing her to prepare the stew under our direction. No woman's rights for him!

Early Monday morning, we prepared to cross Río Yavero and were accompanied to the stream by our Indian host and his entire family. When we reached the bank, there was no canoe or raft in sight. We questioned the Indian, but were unable to gather the import of his reply. Finally he slipped out of his sack-like garment and made motions as if swimming. We gathered from this that he meant for us to swim across the stream, but as it was deep and swift, we entered vigorous objections. Orton, to make the Indian understand that we wanted a boat, quickly opened his pocketknife and whittled out a miniature craft. The Indian nodded vigorously and in turn made a small raft of sticks. When he had completed this, he pointed across the river, indicating that there was a raft on the other side. Having made himself clear, he jumped into the stream, swam across and soon returned with the raft. A glance at the frail craft convinced us that it would carry but one person other than the Indian, and I volunteered to go first. The other side of the stream was reached in safety, though the deck of the raft was slightly under water. As Orton was heavier than I, I shouted to him to send his pack across and then follow. He came across ahead. When the Indian returned alone for Orton's pack and we realized that he could very easily walk off with our belongings, it was with great relief that we saw him place it on the raft and start across the stream.

The Indian led us up a steep bank and pointed out a dim trail leading downstream. We tried in vain to get him to accompany us before finally setting out alone. The trail we had been following on the opposite side of the stream was a cart road compared with the one we were now upon, and it required the utmost watchfulness to keep from going astray. Advancing northwest to a fair-sized river and from there in a northeasterly direction, traveling at times along sheer cliffs that offered scarcely a foothold, we made about seven miles the first day.

We collected wood for our fires just as darkness settled over the land. After eating, we lighted our pipes, but sleep overtook us almost instantly, and we slept the sleep of exhaustion. So keenly had our nerves been tuned by the experiences of the past few days that we awoke at the slightest unusual noise.

The following day the struggle was renewed. We realized fully the consequences of being lost in that almost trackless forest, where not even an Indian was likely to pass for weeks, and we followed the dim trail with increasing vigilance. A short distance from the camp, we lost the way in spite of our extreme care and returned to the camp twice before finally picking up the trail. It led to the trunk of a fallen tree and then disappeared entirely. A fresh-cut branch finally gave us the clue, and we moved forward once more. As we were guided in large measure by openings in the undergrowth, animal trails occasionally led us astray. These invariably ended in a cul-de-sac, and we would retrace our steps to the point of beginning and try another opening.

On the following day we came upon an example of waste that is costing the people of Perú millions of dollars and, unless energetic steps are taken, will eventually wipe out rubber production, one of its greatest industries. Lying directly across the trail was a rubber tree about two feet in diameter that had been felled and "milked" by greedy hunters. The tree had been encircled with deep-cut grooves, about two feet apart, and the milk drawn at these points. We discovered later that felling rubber trees was the general practice throughout the district. The rubber collectors were apparently unconcerned about the future and indifferent to the fact that they were wantonly destroying the greatest source of wealth in this basin. The rubber tree, when cut down and bled at numerous points, yields rich returns, but, of course, no further yield can be obtained from it. The tree from which the rubber is extracted in the conservative manner lives year after year, yielding its milk every season.

After marching an hour beyond the fallen rubber tree, we came to an abandoned camp, quite likely the headquarters of the man who had ruined the great forest giant behind us. The camp had been deserted for some time, but the sight of it was encouraging to us, as it bore witness to the fact that a human being had at one time made his home in this wild, remote section. The rubber trees, which became more numerous as we penetrated the forest, were but one of many examples of splendid forest growth. Red cedar trees, used in the manufacture of canoes in this basin, were abundant. The palm tree also was conspicuously in evidence, as were many varieties of hardwoods.

Birds were numerous, too, but of a limited variety. Parrots of nearly every color and size were seen on every side, but birds of other varieties were scarce. The forest evidently contained many animals, but we rarely caught sight of these. Infrequently, a deer bounded away upon our approach, or a drove of wild hogs crashed through the underbrush. We occasionally saw monkeys, although not so many as expected. While we encountered no other animals, there were numerous signs of their presence.

Near Santa Ana we had seen a number of the deadly coral snakes, beautifully marked with black, red and yellow rings, but since entering the forest, we had seen but one reptile—a small whip-like snake that moved with wonderful rapidity. The absence of snakes was particularly gratifying as we had been cautioned repeatedly by those who pretended to know that we would have to exercise the utmost caution to protect ourselves from the reptiles. We had been told that the snakes of the forest were particularly fond of sharing one's blanket, and in proof of this claim, the fact was pointed out that the forest savages never used blankets. But the chill at night was such that covering was essential to comfort, and we used the blankets regardless of the danger of snakes—a danger that was largely mythical, born, doubtless, of a general ignorance of the forest and what it contained. In truth, those who dwell upon the very edge of this vast region possess only the vaguest knowledge of it. Such knowledge as exists comes from the few savages who occasionally find their way out to barter parrots and monkeys for salt and rum. Señor Tell was the only white man known to have entered the forest, and his experience was held up as a dreadful warning to those who would undertake such a journey.

The windings of the trail on the third day after crossing the Yavero led us across a series of easy hills in a gradual descent to the sandy bed of a small river. When we reached this stream, we found ourselves completely baffled, for search as we would, not a trace of the Indians we were trailing could be found; not a footprint, misplaced stone or broken twig gave any sign. We were lost.

6

⋀⋀⋀

HAVING MADE a thorough canvass of the situation, we decided to follow a small stream until we came to the main river. There we would build a raft for floating downstream until we reached someplace where we could gain a clear idea of our surroundings. We camped that night at the point where the trail disappeared and, on the following day, began our trek along the stream, an extremely difficult undertaking. The footing was poor at best, and at times, on account of the depth and swiftness of the stream, we found it necessary to cut our way through the heavy undergrowth that lined the bank on either side. After seemingly infinite labor we reached the main river and, after making our camp, prepared to build the raft. Food had become a pressing problem by this time, and, in order that we might be able to work on the raft without interruption, we undertook to lay in a supply that would be sufficient for several days. The net result of the afternoon's hunt was a hog, and we smoked the animal that night.

The following morning, just as we were preparing to go hunting again, hopeful that we would land a deer this time, several savages emerged from the forest about a hundred yards above us and advanced in our direction. We immediately went forth, guns in hand, to meet them, and when they came within speaking distance, they halted and signaled us to do likewise. The savages, three in number, were armed with bows and arrows, and decorated with brilliant red paint, but they seemed peaceably inclined. We could not understand their motive for halting us, for they made no attempt to explain their conduct. While we stood in some perplexity, a half-breed appeared and informed us that an aged Spaniard who lived in this region had learned of our presence in the neighborhood through some of his wandering savages and was anxious for us to visit his home. The savages whom we first met were commissioned to extend the hospitalities of the forest home rather than make war upon us.

We accepted the invitation gladly and were soon on the march, relieved of our packs by our guides. By noon we were at the ferry leading to the home of Señor Pereira, and when we landed on the river's opposite shore, an aged man, bearing unmistakable marks of long residence apart from his fellows, welcomed us. "I learned that two white men were near," he said, "and when told that no savages were accompanying them, I was surprised and thought perhaps assistance was needed." We thanked him heartily for his kind invitation and for the interest that prompted him to send for us.

"Did you come through the forest without Indians to guide you?" he asked.

"Yes, señor," we replied.

"Marvelous" was his terse comment.

We explained that the Indians employed to guide us had deserted and that we had followed their trail. Our host, a Spaniard by birth, then invited us to spend a day or two at his home.

Isolated from his own race and color, this aged man has lived for more than forty years among the savages of this wilderness, and for nearly eleven years he had not been thirty miles from the portals of his dwelling. Why he was there he did not say; perhaps behind his life of long retirement there was a dramatic story of a revolution that failed its purpose, or perhaps some darker tragedy over which he wished to draw the veil of obscurity. Again it might have been a tragedy of the heart, some Spanish girl awakening harmonies in the breast of this man when the heart was young and full of fervor. Then, having played love's tune to the accompaniment of languid eyes and bewitching smiles, she may have passed on to other pleasures, leaving him to fight the battle of forgetfulness.

Yet the lot of our host, whose life mystery opened up an endless field for speculation, was not an unenviable one. He seemed to have an unlimited number of savages at his command and was supported in endless ease by these obedient servants. A petty ruler, he lived with his forest children, far from the rush, the endless striving and the ceaseless heart burnings of the outer world. The two nearest cities were Cuzco and Iquitos: the former three hundred miles by trail, a difficult and dangerous journey, as we could testify; the latter, a journey of a thousand miles by launch. Even when one or the other of these cities was reached, the traveler was barely within the circle of civilization.

From whatever motive, Señor Pereira chose well when he determined to bury himself as far as possible from the outer world. He displayed some interest in what was going on there, yet not as much as one would expect. He seemed to realize that vast changes had come about, changes that he would never see or comprehend, for the sands of his life had run full long and soon he would sleep beneath the trees that had sheltered him for four decades.

After breakfast on the morning following our arrival, our host invited us into his private apartment, saying he had a wonderful musical instrument he would be glad for us to examine, although it refused to play. To our amazement he produced a phonograph—a cheap instrument of a type that suggested the early struggles of the inventor. We found that it merely needed a slight adjustment of the diaphragm, and in a short time it was producing music from his very limited stock of records. His servants had collected in the doorway, gazing at the instrument with all wonder, and some of the bolder ones came in and gazed down the horn. The instrument had gotten out of order shortly after its arrival, and only a few of them had ever heard it. While they were jabbering, our host asked, "Do you understand what they say?"

"No, señor, our knowledge of their dialect is too limited," Orton replied.

"They are convinced that there is a very small person in the box," he said, "but they are unable to explain how the little fellow gets along without food or drink, and remains always concealed."

At this moment one of the savages who had picked up a record that had been laid aside for a moment, snapped it in two, evidently expecting to find something inside it. Our host promptly cuffed his ears and ejected him from the room. The phonograph, which would cost about $25 ordinarily, was brought from Cuzco at a cost of $350, and it was evident that Señor Pereira felt he was getting value received despite the limited number of records on hand.

We brought ravenous appetites to our host's table. Aware of the hunger-producing effects of a trip such as ours, he constantly urged us to satisfy our cravings regardless of appearances. After eating we would rest upon seats placed at a point overlooking the river and talk of the mysteries of the forest and of the deeper mysteries of human nature as portrayed in different parts of the world. Señor Pereira admitted that a visit to that outer world he used to know so well would be like an awakening from a Rip Van Winkle sleep.

Our intended stay of a single day lengthened into three, and on the fourth morning, accompanied by a guide furnished by our host, we set out for the rubber camp to which the fugitive guides were to have led us. The picture of our host as we took our departure is vividly impressed on my mind. Dressed in the simple attire of a savage he stood in the low, vine-clad doorway, his shoulders bent under the weight of years, and waved a regretful farewell to the two white men who in all probability would be the last of his own color his eyes would ever behold. Our coming had been an event in his life, and no doubt its loneliness was accentuated by our departure.[1]

When we approached a ford on Río Sanriato,[2] across which our way led, a tapir, one of the immense amphibious animals found in this section, floundered out of the stream and dashed through the undergrowth, carrying all before it, with a crashing sound that could be heard for a hundred yards. When these animals stampede in numbers they tear through vines, crush the undergrowth and carry down saplings, leaving a trail clear of all but the larger trees.

From Río Sanriato, the trail, after a short, sharp ascent, gradually led downhill to Río Guayato.[3] "What is the distance to Malanquiato?"[4] we asked as we halted before fording the Guayato.

"Four leagues, señor," answered the guide.

Twelve miles was not considered a great distance, but the most difficult part of the journey was just ahead, it being necessary to scale a mountain that was quite steep. We pointed out the difficulties to the guide and suggested that we spend the night at the base. He insisted, however, that it was only three miles to the summit and that we could get there before nightfall without difficulty. We moved forward, but soon found that our idea of the difficulties ahead was not far wrong. At times we were forced to climb hand over hand, holding to roots and branches, and at others moved along the sheer face of cliffs that offered barely purchase enough for the toes. One false step meant certain death, and we moved with the utmost caution. Long before the dangerous and difficult climb had been completed, the shades of night began to gather, and we realized that there was no possibility of reaching the summit. We halted for the night at the first favorable spot.

The deftness and rapidity with which the guide erected the shelter of palm leaves was a revelation to us. Within thirty minutes he had completed a typical Indian wickiup[5] capable of turning the hardest tropical downpour. We slept soundly until about midnight, when the report of a gun brought us to our feet with a bound. Our guide, who stood with the smoking gun in his hand, informed us that an animal of some kind had attempted to enter the camp and he had fired upon it. We were disturbed a second time and informed that the animal had been prowling around again. Alarmed at the boldness of the animal, we took turns at watching throughout the remainder of the night, but were not again disturbed.

A climb of two hours in the morning light took us to the summit at a point overlooking the Pongo Rapids,[6] two thousand feet below. The river was about six hundred feet in width above the rapids, but forced its way between perpendicular cliffs not more than a hundred feet apart at this point, and the roar of waters as they rushed through this narrow defile could be heard at a great distance. After leaving the gorge, the river appeared to follow a serpentine course, almost doubling on itself at times, until it vanished into the forest—a level expanse of green reaching toward the eastern confines of the Amazon basin. On the western side of the stream, the forest continued for fully fifty miles to the foothills of the Andes.

The region in which we now stood, and that wider expanse over which our eyes roamed with lively interest, is marked on the official Peruvian map as "unknown" and "unexplored," and as inhabited by *chunchus* [forest dwellers]. The explorations made by the *caucheros*[7] [rubber gatherers] is the only source of information concerning this wilderness, and, with these explorations having been confined to the banks of the streams, the government has no accurate knowledge of what the region contains. There is a common conviction that hostile tribes live in these unknown depths, prepared to resist any invasion.

About five miles down the river we could outline the rubber station of Puerto Mainique[8] with its palm-thatched huts on either side of the stream. After two hours' descent we saw cups attached to the rubber trees for catching the rubber that flows from the bleeding wounds in the bark. The modern method of spiral and herringbone tapping was apparently unknown in the Amazon basin; incisions were made in a primitive fashion using a chisel-pointed hatchet with a cup attached to catch the drip. Soon after passing the *estradas,* the lots of a hundred trees that are tapped every other day, we came to the coagulating camp and, in a banana patch near the river about a mile farther on, reached the building of the manager of the station. We found him engaged in eating breakfast, but when he saw us approaching, he stopped immediately and ran forward with evident delight. He told us that we were welcome to all the camp afforded, but that he was out of tea, coffee, sugar and medicine.

"However," he added, "I have sent for supplies, and they should arrive at any moment."

We then told him that we had employed his Indians as guides and that they had deserted us.

"Very unaccountable, their non-arrival," he commented, with evident surprise.[9]

We presented him with sufficient tea to meet his personal needs for some time to come and were soon enjoying a hearty breakfast of bananas and yuca root, with a brew of our tea.

"Now, what's the news?" was the question fired at us as soon as we were comfortably seated at the table.

This was the invariable question whenever we met a white man during the trip. To a person living in the wilderness for months, and sometimes years, the advent of a visitor is an occasion long to be remembered. It means temporary relief from a monotonous grind, an infusion of fresh ideas and topics, and a brief respite from conditions that have become nerve-racking. This manager, a man of some education and worldly experience, was compelled to associate day after day with men who have never known anything but a condition of semi-savagery. Aside from the daily occupations of collecting rubber, the manager and his men had no ideas in common, and the employment itself was not sufficient to occupy his mental faculties.

Some men go mad under such conditions, and it is the custom with the larger companies managed by European executives to require their chiefs to return home at least once every three years. This prevents mental starvation and keeps the bold spirits who direct this work from falling victims to the madness of isolation.

Informed of our intention to build a raft and float to the head of navigation,[10] the chief offered to point out the balsa tree,[11] the timber the natives use in constructing such crafts. "But," he continued, "there is no occasion for haste. The rainy season is nowhere near, and you must remain here until you've thoroughly recovered from the fatigue of your journey."

The following day, late in the afternoon, as I sat quietly smoking on the bank of a small stream near the camp, a wild pig crossed the stream. With the report of my gun, it dropped, and that night we would enjoy barbecued pork. A little while later, I heard voices and watched an Indian armed with bow and arrows came into view, followed by a squaw. Upon reaching the stream, the squaw entered the water and, after splashing about for a short time, raised a large stone and dashed it against other stones in the water. She repeated this a number of times and almost invariably picked up a small fish that had been killed by the concussion. I watched the woman for fully half an hour as she gathered several pounds of fish by this unusual method. The process seemed simple, but proved a complete failure when I tried it later.

Near the mouth of the small stream in which I had made ineffectual efforts to catch fish Indian-fashion, the manager pointed out the balsa tree, and we began the construction of our raft.[12] Eight of these trees, which are remarkably light and buoyant, were felled and carried to the main stream, where they were left for two days to dry. In the meantime we fashioned long pins from palm wood to fasten the logs together. The work of cutting these pins was very difficult. Orton was in favor of simply lashing the logs together with vines after the native style, but I persuaded him to stick to the task and thereby make the raft as substantial as possible. That we exercised care in making the frail raft would frequently be a matter of congratulation when we encountered fierce rapids later on. When the raft was finally completed, Orton contemplated it with vast satisfaction, saying, "We will travel comfortably now." Carrying fifty pounds over the rough forest trail had not been a pleasant experience for either of us.

While the raft was being built, we went on an occasional hunting trip in order to relieve the monotony of boiled bananas and yuca root. On one of these expeditions I lost my bearings while trying to get a shot at a wild hog, and, attempting a shortcut to the station, I discovered that I had gone farther down the river than intended. Instead of immediately retracing my steps, I tried to advance along the river and soon became hopelessly entangled in a swampy growth. Realizing the futility of attempting to reach the camp by this course, I turned back, hoping to reach some elevated point from which I could get my bearings. In making a sudden turn I came upon a huge snake, fully twelve feet in length, which displayed every indication of disputing the way. The reptile was not more than ten feet from where I stood, and when my gun, brought into hasty action, exploded twice in rapid succession, the heavy shot tore the head of the reptile almost from its body. The terrible contortions through which the great body went as it writhed among the undergrowth was not a nerve-quieting sight, and I left the scene none too leisurely. Reaching an elevated point after about an hour, I got my bearings and had no further difficulty in reaching the camp. The snake I killed was undoubtedly a boa constrictor, though not many of these reptiles had been seen about the camp.

On the following night the barking of the station dog aroused us, and when we made an investigation, we heard a noise in the underbrush, which the chief declared was made by the movement of one of these huge serpents. The next morning we found ample evidence of the presence of such a monster in the neighborhood of the camp, but our efforts to find it were unavailing. The camp lacked much in being a healthful place, so I suggested the chief move the station to higher ground. This would, of course, entail considerable trouble, and he did not think it worthwhile to make the change. Rubber gatherers seem to accept fever and ague[13] as a matter of course. When precautions are suggested, they say, "All rubber men have the fever and ague," and let it go at that.

On the seventh day after beginning our raft, we launched it and found that it met all our expectations as to buoyancy and capacity. We then made preparations for an immediate departure, fearful lest further delay might result in our being caught in the forest by the rainy season. We had hoped to purchase some tobacco at this station, but in this we were disappointed. However, we obtained a native leaf that made a fair substitute for the genuine weed. Our host also provided us with sufficient bananas and yuca root to last several days, and was on hand with most of his associates to bid us a regretful farewell when our craft swung out into the stream. The river was about 200 yards wide at this point, its current running near the opposite shore. As we poled out into its flow, the onlookers cheered lustily and called out some final words of farewell and good cheer. A moment later we were caught in the swift current and carried from the view of the kindly chief and his considerate helpers.

Repeated assurances had been given us that the river was perfectly safe below the Pongo Rapids, and we anticipated an enjoyable experience as we glided gently down the stream. Our expectations received a rude shock, however, for we had not been on the stream an hour before it sprang one of its unpleasant surprises upon us. We noticed that the stream narrowed abruptly and seemed to fairly leap forward, and when we rounded a sudden bend, the cause was clear. Like a mighty millrace, the waters surged between the perpendicular walls of a narrow pass, and a moment later we were borne along at a mad rate, barely missing destruction more than once as we shot by huge boulders protruding above the hurrying waters.

After this exciting experience, the river was comparatively calm for about two miles; then again our ears were greeted with the roar of another rapids. In this instance, we grounded, carried our cargo around the rapids and hauled the raft around through some shoals.

Then followed numerous experiences like that mad journey through the first rapids. In most instances, the forest embraced the very edge of the stream, and the undergrowth was so thick that it was impossible to land. Thus we were balked in any desire we might have had to make a sort of portage[14] and get the raft through as best we could. So, with no other alternative before us, we rushed into one series of rapids after another until after four o'clock in the afternoon, when we came to a sandbar and camped there for the night. After supper, we discussed the situation over our pipes and consoled ourselves with the reflection that we had been passing through a part of the Pongo Rapids and that the worst was over.

The following morning, we made an early start, but had not gone far before the dull roar of troubled waters came to us. We knew that another trying experience was near at hand. The speed of the water became greater, and the roar just ahead almost drowned our voices. At a point where the river turned almost at right angles we saw a great whirlpool in which the waters churned in fury, and we made almost superhuman efforts to avoid it. Closer and closer we were drawn within the restless circle of the whirlpool and a moment later were fairly caught. We swept around swiftly but smoothly until we came in contact with the inflowing water from above. Then the raft, careening almost over, was tossed back into the hurrying circle of the whirlpool. Around and around we went, and our efforts to paddle into the outrush were without the slightest effect. Finally we circled close enough to the overhanging bank to grasp some roots and get ashore using the mooring vine. It was not difficult then to tow the raft out of the whirlpool, so we circled as far as possible from the danger point, after making a start at a place as far above the rapids as possible. But the influence of that whirlpool was irresistible. We were drawn into it a second time despite our most dedicated efforts.[15]

Realizing the futility of attempting to get by the whirlpool from the upper side, we decided to try to land on the opposite side of this furious vortex of water. It fell to my lot to make the leap from the raft to the shore when it approached close enough in its sweep around the pool, and I was again successful in securing a safe hold upon the hanging roots. Clinging to the mooring vine, I swerved the raft out of the pool and Orton leaped ashore. Cutting a long vine, we fastened it to the other vine and prepared to pull the raft into the outrush to the quieter waters below. Before attempting this, however, we removed our packs as a matter of precaution, having lost all of the bananas and other food when the raft tilted upon entering the whirlpool. Had our packs not been securely fastened to the raft, we would have also lost them. While we were making preparations to remove the packs, Orton dislodged a large stone from the bank, and it crashed down upon the raft, barely missing me and striking my pack full force. This seemed a trivial matter at the time, but it would prove to be serious enough when the full extent of the damage was discovered.

When everything was in readiness to pull the raft into the outrush, we decided it would be necessary for one of us to get on the craft while the other slacked away on the vine, as it would not do to run the risk of losing the only means of transportation at hand. Orton agreed to ride the raft while I manipulated the rope. Our scheme worked fine in so far as getting into the outrush was concerned, but when the raft was fairly caught by the swirling current, the vine to which I was clinging parted, and Orton, aboard the raft, was swept rapidly down the stream. He passed from view a few minutes later and I was left on the bank of that wild river far from the haunts of man.

7

WITH THE DISAPPEARANCE of the raft, I realized that my only chance of escape was in following the stream, since it would be utterly impossible for Orton to pole the unwieldy craft upstream against such a current. But to follow it was not an easy matter. Without a craft of some kind, the river was impossible, while the forest growth, which extended to the very edge of the stream, offered an almost impassable barrier. Yet this seemed the only way, so with rifle in one hand and machete in the other, I attacked the undergrowth. Progress was slow, painful and tedious. The way was obstructed at every foot by tangled vines, rank weeds, stubborn palms and other tropical growth. At the end of an hour, I had advanced only about two hundred yards. In the meantime, Orton could easily have been swept down the stream a distance of six or eight miles. Buoyed by the hope that he had succeeded in making a landing at some nearby point, I continued to cut and slash, and after two hours of toil, was rewarded by hearing the voice of my companion calling from about a hundred yards distant. Presently I could hear the sound of another machete's swip-swip and realized that Orton had landed and was cutting through the undergrowth in search of me. When we met, I learned that he had landed about half a mile below and, as soon as he made the raft secure, had started back in an effort to join me, cutting his way just as I had.

Returning to where the packs had been left, we carried them to the craft and, lashing them on, set forth once more. The stream was ominously quiet for a long stretch, and then our ears were assailed by the dull roar of rushing waters. We passed through the next rapids without disaster and reached another smooth stretch. Here we lighted our pipes and prepared to take things easy for a time, but before the contents of the pipes had been half consumed, we were swept into a noiseless but rapid stretch in which the river seemed to pass over a long series of terraces. The waves ran almost as high as our heads, and we were bounced up and down as if out at sea. Our raft rode the waves beautifully, and we rather enjoyed this experience when we found that the danger from rocks was not so great. But our joy was short-lived. A bend in the river marked the end of the terrace-like stretch, and we were swept into another whirlpool almost before we realized what was happening. Here we went through a repetition of our former experience. Around and around, and every effort to steer out of the circle proved in vain. It seemed that we were doomed to spend our lives circling that whirlpool. At last, seizing the end of the mooring vine, I leaped into the water at the point nearest land and succeeded in getting ashore. The raft was then pulled shoreward and tied securely. As in the former case, we were on the upper side of the whirlpool and it was necessary to devise some means of getting through. Throwing a piece of wood into the extreme outer circle of the whirlpool, we watched the result. After making three or four circuits of the pool, it was caught in the out-rush and swept downstream. Hopeful that the raft would do likewise, we launched forth. Fully a dozen times we were carried around the pool, but failed to escape, even though we paddled desperately when the out-rush was reached.

By this time, the sun was not over a half-hour high, and it looked very much as if we would have to spend the night circling the suckhole, as there was no place on the steep bank where we could camp. As a last desperate resort, I took the vine rope and leaped as far into the out-rush as I could get when the raft swept around to that point. Luckily, I landed against a rock, gained a footing and, with great effort, succeeded in pulling the raft after me. Caught by the rushing waters, it swept past me. I leaped for it, but barely struck the end and tumbled off into the water. Clinging to the vine, I was carried along in the wake of the raft, in peril of being dashed against the rocks. I finally succeeded in working my way, hand over hand, to the raft and aided in making a landing at a point on the opposite side of the stream several hundred feet distant.

The hurried darkness was gathering about us now, and we barely had time to collect wood for a fire when the dull gray of evening gave way to the blackness of night. We were soaking wet and hungry as well, and the loss of all our food was keenly felt. This presented a vital problem and caused us no little concern. We thought, of course, that sufficient game could be found to keep us alive, but hunting would mean the loss of time. We had seen wild hogs, parrots and other game along the river, but it was useless to shoot from the raft. The game, if killed, would be left far behind before we could make a landing. In discussing the events of the last two days, we were ready to admit the apparent tranquility of the river, as viewed from the summit above the Pongo Rapids, was a delusion. The names we called the Indians who had informed us that it was not at all dangerous would scarcely look well in cold type.

Fresh tracks near the water the next morning indicated that the larger animals of this section were nocturnal. The tapir, one of the most familiar of the night prowlers, could be heard every night, swimming about in the inlets of the river. The impression of their three-toed front feet encircled our camping place, showing that they had been making an inspection while we slept undisturbed. About noon, we came upon a deserted Indian camp. We were successful in landing at this point and explored the area with a view to finding food of some kind. Our only reward was a bunch of unripe bananas, scarcely fit for food. The vegetable banana[1] grows almost exclusively in this basin; sweet bananas are seldom seen.

At one of the huts in this abandoned camp, I found a human skull near what had been a roasting platform—a structure made of bamboo and elevated sufficiently from the ground to allow anything placed on it to be cooked by fire without danger to the rack or the meal. Scattered about the place were other parts of a human skeleton. At that time I thought perhaps the body of some dead person had been cremated, but some months afterward I mentioned it to a pioneer rubber man—one who had spent the greater part of his life in the forests bordering the rivers—and he assured me that it was the deserted camp of a band of cannibal savages. He said none of the forest tribes ever cremated their dead, that they either threw the body into the river or ate it. Many others who had been long in this portion of Perú related stories of cannibalism, and there seems to be no doubt that the savages in the heart of the great rubber belt practice it.[2]

The following brief entry appears in my notebook on the date following our landing at the cannibal camp: "Character of the river unchanged; sluggish stretches followed by rapids. Suffering from hunger." I recall this day distinctly because the distance between the rapids had been greater than on the preceding days. But whenever we encountered an unusually long stretch of smooth river, we made preparations for an extremely rough passage through the next rapids. The rule seemed to hold good that the greater the distance of smooth passage, the more violent the rapids. An encounter with rapids invariably left us as wet as if we had plunged into the stream, but the intensity of the tropical sun quickly dried our clothing as we floated lazily from one rapids to another. The western bank of the river was of rocky formation and numerous stones, huge and flat, were seen in the stream, some raising their heads high above the prevailing water level. The eastern bank was low lying and generally level, with a rank growth of trees, cane, grass and vines, the whole forming an almost impenetrable barrier. At some places where the bank of the stream was unusually high, markings could be seen fully forty feet above the present level, and we were duly impressed with the thought of what a mighty stream this became when the rainy season set in and the water began pouring down from the mountains with irresistible force. Having been repeatedly warned not to get caught on this river during the rainy season, each day carried the force of this timely advice home to us.

As we had been practically without food for forty-eight hours, we landed at an unusually early hour in the afternoon and attempted to bag some game. We scouted all around the sandbar upon which the raft had been anchored, but were unable to find even so much as a parrot. With the approach of darkness, we were forced to give up empty-handed and busy ourselves in getting wood for a fire. It was absolutely necessary for us to have a fire if the hunters were to escape being the hunted. Wild animals have a wholesome dread of fire, and, no doubt, we owed our security on many occasions to the fact that the fire was never allowed to die out entirely. Time and again we had awakened in the morning to find that wild animals had paraded around us while we slept, but never at any time were we molested.

At this camp I suffered an attack of ague,[3] the first experienced in South America. Liberal use of the medicinal rum, together with quinine, modified subsequent attacks. Orton also suffered ague from this time forward, but refused to take the rum mixture.

Our distress from lack of food now began to be acute, and this, combined with the recurring chills, began to tell upon our physical condition. Although surrounded by game, we were so situated that it was impossible to kill any, and as day after day had passed without relief, we were face to face with starvation. To add to the gloom of the situation, at least so far as I was concerned, Orton seemed to constantly dwell on some great feast he had enjoyed in times past. He would tell over and over of a splendid dinner eaten at Melbourne or a feast that was prepared for him some other place. Although absolutely without anything to eat, he was at least determined to talk of eating. In the meantime, I was trying to keep my mind off the subject, and it was with many sharp words that I interrupted his conversation when it turned to the good things he had enjoyed in that far outer world—a world that seemed to grow more dim and distant with each passing day.

On the fifth day that we had been without food, we landed at a point where a small stream flowed in from the forest. While I made ready for the night, Orton went in search of game, just as he had done day after day. I felt and he felt that a crisis was coming and that it would end disastrously unless we obtained food in a very short time. To fast when taking no exercise is hard enough, but it becomes doubly hard when every energy has to be put forth throughout the day. We were ravenous. When suddenly the deep silence of the forest was broken by the roar of his gun, my heart leaped into my throat. Presently Orton approached through the gathering shadows with two dark objects in his hands. Oh, joy, a roast, I thought, but my pleasure was dulled considerably when I realized the animals were nothing more nor less than monkeys.

"I can't eat monkey," I said.

"I could eat one of them raw" was Orton's laconic reply, as he began skinning one.

When the animals had been cooked, I enjoyed my first meal of monkey. Although the meat was tender and wholesome, the word *enjoyed* is used advisedly. I was almost starved and consumed half of one of the monkeys. Orton not only ate the other half but the other monkey as well.

Impressions in the sand about this camp showed it to be the watering place of wild animals. At one spot, the earth was torn up by what had evidently been a fierce encounter between a jaguar and some other ferocious animal, the nature of which we could not determine. Throughout the night animals prowled about, growling threateningly at times, but we were thoroughly exhausted and willing to trust our fire for protection, To have attempted to kill one of the animals for food would have been useless, as they kept within the impenetrable darkness where it would have been pure folly to venture.

Just after we pushed the raft off the shore on the following morning and before it had been caught by the current, I spotted a ronsoco[4] not twenty feet away. These animals resemble domestic hogs and weigh about a hundred pounds when fully grown. This one seemed a providential gift. Hastily unstrapping my rifle from the raft, I jerked it into position and fired. The ronsoco looked around with a grunt of surprise and retreated into the forest. The animal was so near that a miss seemed impossible, and it took several seconds for me to grasp the fact that I had touched neither hide nor hair of the much-coveted ronsoco.

The high-strung state to which Orton and I had been brought by hunger and hardship was clearly demonstrated after my bad shot. We quarreled over it and argued about it like a couple of angry fisherwomen. This is not an uncommon experience. Two men thrown together for weeks, having no other companionship, frequently get on one another's nerves, and arguments prolonged and heated occur frequently. With nerves on edge, they are ready to resent things that would pass unnoticed under ordinary circumstances. Such disputes mean nothing, though, for with rest and recreation, hasty differences are forgotten and the bonds of friendship become more firmly welded by reason of mutual hardship and suffering.

Our daily life had by this time settled down to an almost unvarying routine. With the first appearance of dawn, we would arise, boil water for tea, and, if by chance, a monkey or parrot had fallen victim to our guns, we would broil a sufficient quantity for our breakfast and midday lunch. Then we would return to the river, always with a vague sense of uneasiness, haunted by the fear that, perhaps unknown to us or our advisers, there was a waterfall somewhere along the treacherous stream that would carry us to our death. About four o'clock in the afternoon we would begin looking out for a suitable place to spend the night. Upon making a landing, one would hunt while the other arranged the camp. If morning ablutions were forgotten or neglected when the start was renewed, the first rapids would mitigate the offense.

Two or three days after what had now become known as the "hog incident," I was cleaning my rifle and discovered that the barrel was hopelessly bent. The heavy rock that had tumbled upon my pack when we were caught in the first whirlpool had struck the weapon midway between the lock and the muzzle. I attempted to straighten the muzzle, but met with no success. Thereafter it was effective only at very close range, and I lost all confidence in it. It was ruined forever as an accurate firearm. Up to this time the injury to my rifle was the most serious accident of the journey, a reliable firearm being the most necessary equipment for a trip through the wilds. Fortunately, Orton's shotgun, an excellent magazine weapon, was in good order, and we also had six-shooters, which were effective at close range.

Frequently, as we floated down the stream through places where the water was smooth, we attempted to catch some fish with hook and line. Fish were all about us, an infinite variety, but our knowledge of how to cater to their whimsical taste was sadly deficient, and we never got so much as a bite. This was truly remarkable in view of the great number of fish we saw and the perfect freedom with which they swam about the raft at times. After many attempts to entice them with bits of meat and worms, we came to the conclusion that they were vegetarians.

Mishahua[5] now became the magic word. We should have reached this camp in three or four days after leaving the rubber settlement far up the river, but our informants knew as little of the camps along the stream as they did of its turbulent nature. At Mishahua, we expected to satisfy all our longings for food—a subject upon which our thoughts now dwelt the greater part of the time.

One misty morning, while we were breaking camp, several jaguars roared a defiant challenge from the jungle across the river, but their close proximity aroused no apprehension, though the black variety is said to be the most ferocious of South American animals. Above the Pongo we had seen an Indian with maimed and useless hands, the result, it was said, of an encounter with a black jaguar. According to the story told, and to which his distorted hands bore witness, he and another Indian were walking along a forest trail when attacked. As the ferocious animal sprang at him, he thrust both hands into its open mouth. While the jaguar held his hands imprisoned, the other Indian killed it. We saw the skin of this half-grown animal at the home of Señor Pereira, our friend of the forest, who vouched for the story.

Whenever we camped near a thick growth of cane, great numbers of paroquets[6] circled around, chattering as they prepared to settle for the night. In the morning, with the first streaks of dawn, they were up, screaming and scolding as they winged their flight to the feeding grounds. Macaws, long tailed, large headed, brilliantly plumed birds, were also numerous. They flew in pairs, circling about at a great height until the sun dropped low, then they would disappear into the forest. The macaw, which feeds on berries and flowers found in treetops and at other high points, is extremely shy, yet if one of a pair is shot, the uninjured bird follows the wounded one in its sudden drop to the earth, screaming the while as if attempting to persuade it to turn again toward the blue of the sky. Because of this trait, the experienced hunter, after killing one of these birds, always stands ready to bag the other.

We had now been on the river for over two weeks and were greatly perplexed as to the whereabouts of Mishahua. At times we feared that we had passed it and would rack our brains in an effort to recall some bit of scenery that would suggest the proximity of a camp. All our efforts were in vain; we had seen no such place. Moreover, we had not encountered a human being in all that long voyage, nor seen any evidence of human habitation beyond the deserted camp of the cannibal Indians.

Frequently while passing through this wild and lonely section, we commented upon the fact that we had not been disturbed at any time by savages, tales of whose cruelty were numerous beyond the borders of the great forest in which they made their home. One of these stories, a fair sample of the many, was to the effect that a young engineer ventured into the haunts of these people and was gone so long that friends became alarmed and organized a search party. They found him finally, so the story went, tied to a tree, just the remnant of a man. The Indians had cut off his limbs—choice parts, it was said—and left him there to die.[7] Stories of this kind were not pleasant to hear, nor to recall as we made our meager preparations to sleep at night. We congratulated ourselves time and again that we had not encountered any such race, the Indians with whom we had come in contact having treated us with every consideration.

8

$\wedge\wedge\wedge$

OUR FIRST ENCOUNTER with hostile tribesmen occurred several days after the discovery that my rifle had been damaged. Throughout each night, the fire required attention about every two hours, and as the increasing dampness warned us that the logs were burning low, we took turns keeping them ablaze. On this night, Orton arose to tend to the fire and, a moment later, called out, not loudly but distinctly, "Get up quick." I threw away the blanket and instinctively reached for my rifle when the sharp swish, swish of speeding arrows fell upon my ears. "Indians!" we both exclaimed, and at that moment, as I hurriedly arose from an all-four position, one of the arrows passed beneath my body.

We backed as speedily as possible from the firelight, retreating towards the river. At the same time, we directed a sweeping rifle fire towards the jungle, from which the arrows had come. Near the riverbank, beyond our fire's circle of light, we crouched, expecting any moment to see the Indians emerge from the jungle and attempt to overpower us. All was silent, and after the first excitement of the attack died down, I half wished the Indians would make the rush I felt sure was coming sooner or later. The suspense was worse than actual conflict. My eyes became painfully weary with peering into the darkness, and my limbs were stiff with the chill and dampness of night. It would be impossible to describe with what laggard feet the next hour went by or with what joy we beheld the light of dawn creeping into the eastern sky.

This exchange of shots occurred just about an hour before dawn, the hour savages of this region deem most favorable for beginning an attack. Not an arrow had been fired after the first volley from our weapons swept the undergrowth. Why the Indians, who evidently outnumbered us, did not charge was a matter of speculation, but we came to the conclusion that it was due to our repeating weapons. In all probability the attacking party had never encountered a weapon that continued to belch forth bullets, and the rapid fire had filled them with dismay. As soon as it was light enough to see, we hurriedly pulled our packs aboard the raft and continued our journey. We made no effort to ascertain to what tribe the Indians belonged or how many there were. It was with infinite relief that we departed, satisfied to escape unharmed.

The following forenoon we sighted an Indian camp on the eastern bank of the stream, and, as it presented a peaceful as well as tempting picture, we decided to make a landing. It proved to be the temporary camp of a roving band of Conibos,[1] the male members of which were absent for the time being.

As we approached the wickiup, a squaw, surrounded by children and dogs, glanced up for a moment in stolid indifference and then resumed her efforts to make the fire burn brighter by vigorous fanning. An earthen pot was suspended over this fire, and the smell that came up from it filled us with the happy anticipation of a hearty meal. The lean, hungry dogs were inclined to dispute our approach, but as we disregarded them, they did no more than sniff about our legs.

Addressing the squaw in Spanish, we asked for something to eat. A blank stare was the result. Thereupon we pointed significantly at the steaming pots and at our hungry mouths. This seemingly intelligent effort to convey to her the fact that we were hungry also was ineffectual. The squaw merely grunted and returned to her fanning.

Having exhausted our knowledge of language, both sign and verbal, I stepped forward and lifted the lid from the pot. Inside I beheld a quantity of fish and bananas. Extracting my knife from its sheath, I succeeded in fishing out a banana and was attempting to lift out a fish when the squaw finally arose and produced two earthen bowls. These she filled, handing one to Orton and the other to me. Whatever her thoughts may have been concerning these men with strange faces, tongues and manners, she rightly concluded that she was dealing with two half-starved individuals with whom it might prove unwise to trifle. As we hungrily devoured the bananas and fish, she prepared some yuca root. In the meantime, another squaw sat nearby, attentively stringing beads into a necklace, as indifferent to what was transpiring as though the appearance of two bold and hungry white men was an incident of frequent occurrence—as well as a great nuisance.

Some fish oil, under ordinary circumstances greasy and unpalatable, was served with the boiled yuca root, the arrival of which was the signal for another onslaught. Our capacity for food so impressed the squaw that she wound up bringing forth a stewed bird of formidable size. This, however, was rejected. Eating birds had begun to feel repulsive to me. An unchanging diet of birds and monkeys is likely to have this effect upon anyone.

In an effort to get some light upon the location of the elusive Mishahua, we called out the name repeatedly and at the same time pointed down the river. Doubtless relieved to find that we had not come to spend the rainy season with her, the squaw suddenly developed a remarkable intuition. Pointing to a canoe, she swept her arm from the eastern almost to the western horizon and then pointed to the sun. Our interpretation of her gestures was that Mishahua was a short day's journey by canoe.

As we prepared to take our departure, the squaw, evidently anxious to speed the parting guests, pressed some more food upon us, giving us a generous store of bananas and yuca root from the abundant supply of the camp. In return for her kindness we gave her one of our trading handkerchiefs—a piece of cloth bordered in yellow, red and pink, with an ill-shaped green-colored tiger as a center decoration. This color scheme seemed to conform perfectly to the Indian idea of harmony, although it led me to think the designer had been afflicted with delirium tremens.[2]

The Río Urubamba, on whose murky bosom we were once more adrift, did not improve on acquaintance. The rapids came in quick succession and the stream twisted so that it was difficult to see ahead for any considerable distance. We were swept around sharp bends and carried with swiftness through rapids that more than once threatened the destruction of our frail craft. Late in the afternoon we landed at the deserted camp of a band of rubber gatherers and felt that we were in great good luck, for the palm-thatched huts were in serviceable condition and offered protection from the rain, which had begun to fall and was increasing into a steady downpour.

We built a fire in the end of one of the huts, and I prepared the yuca roots for supper while Orton gathered an additional supply of wood. Presently I heard someone approaching, but paid no attention to the sound, supposing it was Orton returning. I was somewhat startled when a stranger appeared before me with the request, uttered in Spanish, "Permit me, señor, fire please." A rough brown hand was extended, and the half-breed owner continued, "We are camping here."

"We," I said, surprised to learn that there were others in the neighborhood.

"Yes, señor, my patrón and his Indians."

"How far is it to Mishahua?" I asked.

"About five hours," he replied.

Upon the return of Orton, we went to the hut occupied by the patrón and were cordially invited to enter. When he learned that we had come by raft from the Pongo Rapids, he exclaimed, "Wonderful!" We told him something of our experiences on the way, and he said, "I know little of the river, as only Indians venture so far up, but you have undoubtedly passed the most dangerous part of the stream." He insisted on our taking supper with him, and when the meal was over, we smoked and chatted for some time. As we finally took leave of him, he presented us with a smoked fish.

Though we were up bright and early the following morning, the rubber gatherer and his little band of Indians had gone on their way. We resumed our journey with heightened spirits, feeling that before the close of another day we would be in the longueur for Mishahua. We fairly bubbled over with good humor and jolly conversation, our conduct being in marked contrast to that of the preceding day, when the weight of loneliness rested heavily upon us and we felt that, to float on and on down a rough and dangerous stream was apparently to be our lot for the remainder of our lives. This day was not without its perils, however; late in the afternoon, we encountered one of the worst rapids of the entire trip and barely escaped being capsized in a swirling crosscurrent.

Noting a favorable landing place on a sandbar on the opposite side of the river from a small hut and fearing that we would not be able to reach Mishahua before nightfall, we made landing and prepared to spend the night. A few minutes afterwards, we heard several shots and noticed some men on the opposite side of the river beckoning for us to come across. We joined them and accepted their invitation to spend the night at what proved to be a rubber gatherer's camp. Upon inquiry, we learned that the Mishahua post, our long-sought place of succor, had been abandoned. It lay about three miles beyond the mouth of Río Mishahua, an insignificant stream in appearance that flows into the Urubamba about four hundred yards above this camp. Río Mishahua is the gateway from the Peruvian side to the center of activity in the rubber-gathering industry of the Madre de Dios district,[3] at one time the Klondike of rubber collectors.

During the dry months, many patróns with their Indian slaves and half-breed guides pole up in canoes from the river's head of navigation to risk life and health in the search for new fields. The zeal with which they push forward and the courage with which they bear the sufferings and privations imposed by the wilderness remind me of the old days in the States when men risked their all in the hunt for gold among the Indian tribes of the Far West. The same lust for sudden wealth is in evidence here, and when rubber trees are found, the slow method of tapping is ignored. The trees are felled ruthlessly, bled of their contents and left to rot on the ground. As those Indians engaged in gathering rubber are usually owned by the patrón while the half-breeds are paid very small wages, the profits in the business are large. Of their food supply, the patrón furnishes salt and yuca root meal, the Indians provide meat and fish. The average Indian gathers about $800 worth of rubber in the course of a year, working under normal conditions, and in the meantime, his labor and keep cost about $80 to $100. Yet there are many ifs in the rubber business.

When an unworked district is discovered and the trees are plentiful, the success of the venture is assured, unless the savages resent the invasion of their territory to the point of driving the intruders out. There is also another element of danger. It happens sometimes that after the rubber has been gathered and started for the market, snugly packed in the canoes, some of the frail crafts overturn and the cargo is lost. The cargo of an ordinary canoe is two tons, worth about $500 at the present value of rubber, and the loss of a single cargo is a serious blow.

The story was told of one patrón, who worked about a hundred Indians. Through repeated disasters, he had become involved in debt, aggregating over a million dollars. "Yet he hopes to be able to pay it all and pocket a profit in four or five years," our informant said. This unfortunate *cauchero* is thought to be the largest individual collector in the Amazon basin. The average patrón has from twenty to thirty Indians and, in most instances, is backed by some mercantile house that furnishes the supplies and equipment for the expedition. In such cases the patrón must turn over a liberal share of the profits to the house that finances the venture. The average yield of a rubber tree above eighteen inches in diameter is about 150 pounds; this, when the tree is cut down for bleeding. Smaller trees are not considered worth felling and bleeding. In a few years, at the present destructive pace, the small trees will also be in demand.

Our Peruvian map, the best obtainable, was about thirty miles off in fixing the location of Sepahua,[4] the rubber post below Mishahua. This map placed it thirty miles beyond Río Mishahua, but we learned that it was only three hours distant. Upon reaching the mouth of Río Sepahua, we landed, and while Orton arranged the camp, I went in search of the post store. This post was located on the bank of the Sepahua, about a half mile from the main river, and consisted of four roughly constructed palm-wood buildings. Two Iquitos firms kept supplies there during the dry season, trading with Indians and rubber collectors from the surrounding territory. Señor Hosh, the local representative of the house of Guillermo Soza of Iquitos, was in charge of the first building I came to. The tedious preliminary conversation, which must invariably precede the most trivial business transactions in this part of the world, was in progress when Señor Hosh interrupted, "Come and have breakfast; this is the interim of business here; your purchases can be made after siesta."

Except for the fact that it would have been considered grossly discourteous, I would have declined and, for the sake of my hungry companion, attempted to secure the supplies at the other store without loss of time. But not wishing to offend, I accepted. The meal was what a visitor might expect to sit down to in a typical German home anywhere outside the circle of civilization. My appreciation was apparent; my only regret was the absence of Orton.

The presence of a smokestack about sixteen inches in diameter in front of the store excited my curiosity, and to my questions, Señor Hosh replied, "The stack was discarded by a launch belonging to my firm. The launch passed up Río Mishahua about seven months ago en route to Río Manú. It reached the headwaters, which are separated from the Manú headwaters by a very narrow barrier, too late to take advantage of the high water and is at present being slowly moved upstream by means of temporary locks. About fifty Indian slaves are slowly but surely moving the launch toward the barrier by constructing temporary dams of sandbags. With luck it will be ready to take advantage of the next high water on Río Manú. When it reaches the barrier, it will be taken apart and transferred by land to a suitable place for rebuilding on the Manú. There it will be put together and used on Río Madre de Dios."

The difficult nature of the task undertaken by this company in floating the launch up to the barrier and then transporting it overland will be better appreciated when it is stated that it requires twenty days of poling to convey a canoe to the barrier. To move the launch by temporary locks was a matter of months, aside from the fact that afterwards it had to be taken apart, transported across land and reassembled on the headwaters of the Manú. Only in a country where the price of labor is largely regulated by the quantity of rum on hand could such an undertaking be carried through with any prospect of profit.[5]

"During the high water," continued the agent, "four launches come here from Iquitos. They arrive in January and February, and then for ten months our port is deserted. The nearest port during this long interval is Cumaria,[6] eight days by canoe from here."

If Sepahua ever becomes a city and the current price of necessities remains unchanged, a corner grocery in the place should net the owner a profit sufficient to satisfy the most avaricious. Condensed milk retailed at a dollar per tin and coffee at two dollars per pound. Other goods were sold at proportionate prices. However, the bargain hunter might have fared worse, for in the Madre de Dios district the tin of milk sold in Sepahua for a dollar brings twice as much.

I learned from Señor Hosh that Señor Jorge Robelede, to whom I was the bearer of a letter of introduction from a kinsman at Santa Ana, was in camp not far from the place we had selected to spend the night. We found him and learned that he was on a trading expedition, accompanied only by Indians. The letter I gave him, which seemed to afford him much gratification, was doubtless the last communication he ever received from a member of his family. Two months later, news of his death reached me. When he left us, he went up Río Mishahua to its headwaters. While transferring his merchandise overland to Río Manú, he was ambushed by a band of Amahuacas,[7] a particularly fierce tribe of hostile Indians that are a constant source of danger around the barriers separating Río Sepahua and Río Purus, a large stream flowing into Brasilian territory. A short time after the death of Robelede, two river traders were killed on the Sepahua. Their looted canoes were caught adrift, but no details of the attack were learned.

Just as we were breaking camp at Sepahua, a Chinaman, Antonio Silva by name, came up and addressed us. "Señores," he said, "there is a very dangerous rapids about fifteen hours below here, where the river passes around a small island. Pass to the left of the island and you will go through safely."

We thanked him for this information, and he continued, "I have spent many years on this river and its tributaries. I caution you to be very careful about entering the water from here on. Rayas are numerous.[8] I received this cut years ago," pointing to a sunken scar on the calf of his leg, "and was for many months unable to walk."

As we prepared to push out into the stream, the Chinaman gave us this parting injunction: "Look out for snags about two days this side of Cumaria, for they are numerous and more dangerous than the rapids."[9]

We would learn later that this Chinaman, who displayed such kindly interest in our welfare, was well known on the river, having traded on it for years.[10]

Our next objective was Santa Rosa,[11] where a French expedition was camped. The chief engineer, we learned, was an American, and we anticipated a pleasant interruption in our journey upon reaching this camp. The day after embarking for Santa Rosa was a repetition of many we had experienced since committing our way to the river: Long stretches of smooth water were followed by swift rushes through dangerous rapids. Late in the evening, we landed on a sandbar and camped for the night. From then on, we frequently saw cane wickiups and usually tried to stop at one of these for the night, but were not always successful in landing, for the current sometimes swept us beyond.

The second day below Sepahua, the landscape on the western bank underwent a pleasing change. At places, the foothills came right up to the river, ending so precipitately that they appeared to have been cut off with a great sword, while on the east bank, the expanse was level, uninterrupted by any elevation. Although salt is abundant in the mountains to the west, the tribes living in the forest depths to the east of the river are reputed to be unacquainted with it. When they come under the control of persons to whom salt is a necessity, it is said they must very gradually cultivate the taste.

At this stage of our journey, night birds seemed to be about as numerous as those that filled the forest with song and call during the waking hours. Here, we became acquainted with the "bird of evil men," the *huancahua,* and were regaled by its somber music. The shivery sounds began with the approach of the short tropical twilight, continued through the night and quieted only as dawn was breaking. The Indians of this region wage relentless warfare against this bird, deeming its presence a sure sign of misfortune. The most melancholy sound to greet our ears was the cry of the *taya mama,* a bird with a voice that is almost human. When its cry rings out at night, it sounds as if a child is calling in distress from the depths of the forest. According to the Indians, this cry comes from the soul of a reincarnated child that was slain by its stepparents and whose sobs of pain and sorrow cannot be hushed. It is a cry that gets on the nerves and gives even the most unimaginative person a creepy feeling.[12]

In the quiet stretches of the river, huge bufeo fish came to the surface with a porpoise-like motion, spouted and disappeared. The size and general appearance of these fish is suggestive of danger, but they are perfectly harmless. As they are unfit for food, they are never molested; consequently, they are very numerous. Alligators and turtles were seen frequently, though our appearance was invariably a signal for them to dive into the water and disappear. We occasionally saw otter-like animals that displayed a lively curiosity, would approach quite close to the raft, give an angry bark, much like that of a dog, and then disappear beneath the surface of the water.[13]

About noon on the third day out from Sepahua, we passed the point of confluence of Río Inuya.[14] Extensive groves of rubber trees exist in the territory drained by this stream, but the swift current, dangerous whirlpools and nearly impassable rapids, as well as the presence of Amahuaca tribesmen along its banks, protect the region from rubber gatherers.

9

⌇⌇⌇

THE RAPIDS about which the Chinaman warned us were the most perilous in all this hazardous journey. The river split into three sections and rushed through each division as if in breathless haste to become reunited. We attempted to steer our raft into the left pass, but were unable to do so, were then swept with great speed into the center channel and carried forward at a hair-raising rate. The third division of the stream flowed around a small island and joined the middle division, forming a very dangerous crosscurrent. But our raft, leaping forward like a thing alive, swept on at a rate of at least twenty miles an hour through the swirls of the countercurrents. More than one half the volume of the river rushed through the narrow pass, into which we were carried. That we escaped was due to good luck and not to skill in steering. If we aided the craft, it was through intuition. There was no time for reason.

It had been raining throughout the day, but about four o'clock in the afternoon the sun came out, so we decided to stop at the first favorable camping place and dry out. A part of each day's routine had been the drying of our apparel, for if the rain did not drench us, the rapids did. When we reached camp, we were greeted by the warning notes of the *cacho,* a bird said to be too lazy to build a nest, thus laying its eggs at the most convenient spot on the ground. All is well until rain threatens; then the bird begins to cry in tones of distress, according to native interpretation: "I will build a nest tomorrow, yes, surely build a nest tomorrow." But with the arrival of fair weather, the negligent bird forgets its good intentions, and the nest is never built.[1]

That the *cacho* is a weather prophet, I can testify. We had hardly built a rainproof fire when the rain began again and continued to pour all through the night. We had no time to build a shelter of palms leaves, and throughout the long hours we sat upon our dunnage, ponchos drawn tightly about us, and waited for the downpour to cease. Our dunnage bags, coated with rubber fresh from the trees, were absolutely waterproof, and the rain did no damage except to our feelings. In the murky dawn we took some food and were soon on our way, peering around each bend for a view of Santa Rosa.

About noon we saw an Indian on the riverbank smoking some game on a cane scaffold. We landed and learned through many signs and various markings on the ground that Santa Rosa was just beyond the third bend. The game was a wild hog, and I removed the handkerchief I usually wore around my neck and offered it to him, at the same time pointing to the ham on the smoking scaffold. The exchange was agreeable, and we enjoyed roast wild pork that night, a welcome addition to our larder.

About the middle of the afternoon, we reached the junction of the Tambo and Urubamba rivers and were borne along onto Alto Ucayali.[2]

The country through which Río Alto Ucayali flows is inhabited by hostile members of the Campa tribe. These Indians, rather than become slaves, remain within the depths of the wilderness and live as their forefathers lived. They have not advanced a step since the advent of the Stone Age and manifest not the slightest inclination to depart from their present mode of existence. The territory inhabited by this savage race begins not more than fifteen miles from the junction of the Tambo and Urubamba rivers. It is a region reported to be rich in rubber, but every attempt at invasion meets with stubborn resistance. Some years ago, an unusually bold prospector, who had spent years collecting rubber in the forests of the Amazon basin, decided to venture among them. With this end in view, he camped at the mouth of the Tambo and surrounded himself with friendly Indians and half-breeds. All his overtures were rejected and the newcomers told they must leave the vicinity. When no attention was paid to the warnings, the result was a general attack in which the bold collector barely escaped with his life. Many of his Indians were slain and all of his property destroyed. This incident remains fresh in the popular mind, and since that time, no attempt has been made to invade this territory.[3]

Turning a sharp bend in the river and passing along a straight stretch flowing west, we saw the buildings on the *puesto* [post or station] of Santa Rosa come into view. We landed, and the first person we met was an American engineer.[4] He asked, "Where on earth are you fellows from, the Madre de Dios district?"

"No," we replied, "we're from Lake Titicaca."

When I told him that I left Buenos Aires on January 10, 1907, crossed the Andes, passed through north Bolivia, entered Perú and descended to the present point by raft, he expressed both surprise and regret. "The director-general and others of our party will be disappointed when they learn that you are longer from civilization than we are," he said. "We've been in the interior for months, and I hoped that you would be able to tell us something of what is going on in the world." He insisted upon our remaining for a time with the expedition, saying, "We want to hear your experience. Visits from English-speaking persons are unknown here, and I am delighted to see you."

He was the only English-speaking member of the expedition and, for the benefit of the director-general and others who were not conversant with English and seemed deeply interested in our experiences, we spoke in Spanish. When supper had been disposed of and there was finally a pause in the conversation, the engineer said, "Your Spanish betrays your length of residence in Spanish America, but you have the advantage over a man of Erin who once wandered into Latin America and experienced great difficulty in mastering the native tongue. 'By the saints,' he said, 'it's a curious spache these hathens are after spaking,' and then gave these samples: 'Delaney manes wood [de léna]. McCarty manes rope [mecarte], Kearney manes meat [carne]. Now, I wonder what O'Sullivan manes in this queer tongue.'" This visit was one of the few bright spots in the long journey through the wilds of Perú. To see the faces of white men about us, to hear a joke cracked in our own tongue and to find a friendly interest in our welfare was a pleasure, indeed.

On the following morning, while making some repairs to our raft, we remarked upon its waterlogged condition. The engineer, who remained at our elbows during this brief visit, apparently enjoying every sound of the mother tongue, asked, "On what day did you cut the timber?" We gave the date, whereupon he said, "You felled the tree during the change of the moon, and that accounts for the trouble. Timber cut at that time always rots in a very short time in this basin." We were inclined to look upon this statement in the light of a joke, but he assured us it was true. He had noted it from actual experience.

When we arrived at Santa Rosa, the major portion of the expedition, whose members welcomed us so warmly, was preparing to leave for Cumaria, there to embark on a launch for Iquitos. From Iquitos, they were going to the Argentine. Two days later, as we were about to leave and the members of the expedition were also preparing to get away, a canoe arrived from an engineers' camp up a side stream and brought news that the party there was short of provisions and several members were ill. They had been absent for three months, their exact whereabouts unknown, and great uneasiness had been felt for their welfare. Their condition demanded fitting out a relief expedition, which delayed the departure of those who were to journey down the river. With their change of plan, we remained only long enough to thank our newfound friends for their hospitality. Upon our departure, the American cautioned us: "The rapids themselves aren't very dangerous, but keep a sharp lookout for snags. The river is full of them."

Late in the afternoon we reached Logoto, a notorious slave post.[5] From this point, organized raids are made upon Indians in the Gran Pajonal,[6] and the captives are sold into slavery to rubber collectors. An Indian boy or girl of average size and strength brings about $125 at the age of twelve years. Slaves of this age seem to be preferred, doubtless due to the fact that they are easier to handle and train than older Indians. Once sold into slavery, few Indians ever know anything else. Any hopes they may entertain of again visiting the haunts of their infancy are in vain. They are taken by the purchasers into territory where the savages are unsympathetic, consequently few attempts to escape are made. If they were to desert the camp of the collector, a worse fate would befall them in the hands of hostile Indians.

In the purchase and handling of Indians, the rubber collector displays remarkable ingenuity. He buys only two or three slaves from each tribe, the result being that when he has a large number, they are anything but a harmonious whole. The Indians are never entirely at peace with one another, as intertribal communication and friendship are unknown. It would therefore be impossible to organize a revolt among the slaves. If a few members become unruly, it is not the slightest trouble for the owner to incite the enmity of other slaves and bring about a condition under which the unruly one, if not disposed to childlike obedience, can be speedily put to death by their fellows. The pitting of members of one tribe against the members of another tribe makes the patrón absolute master.

It was at Logoto that the astute Bernanchez, a semi-civilized

Indian, operated a highly successful agency for the distribution of slaves. His plan was to persuade the Indians to venture from the Gran Pajonal and then, when they had fallen into his clutches, hire them out to the rubber collectors at so much per head. He did not actually sell the Indians, but entered into an agreement by which they were to be returned through him to their tribes after working out the term of the contract. Yet few returned, for Bernanchez, as astute as he was, had the usual weakness for cheap finery, and in time he found himself under such obligation to his patróns that he could not always enforce his demand for the return of those he had sold into temporary service. Hearing of his ability to furnish cheap labor and also of his suscepti-bility to "being worked," one river pirate—the owner of a trading launch—attempted to ingratiate himself to Bernanchez by offering to assume all of his debts. With this end in view, he sent one of his agents to see the old rascal. When the invitation was extended, Bernanchez replied, "Humph! Who pays your patrón's debts?"

He was not always so astute as on this occasion and was finally driven from the field by reason of increasing obligations to deliver vassals, who were becoming more and more difficult to obtain as his evil reputation spread and dread of him increased among the forest tribes. But the traffic in slaves did not decrease with the passing of Bernanchez. That post is today the seat of considerable activity in this respect.

A few miles below Logoto we were carried into the Vuelta del Diablo,[7] or "Devil's Bend," a whirlpool formed by an obstruction of sandstone jutting out at a point where the river turns almost at right angles. This whirlpool, dangerous at all times, becomes so menacing during the high water that launches are compelled to wait until the river subsides before attempting to get by it. When we were brought with a rush into its grip, it seemed for a few minutes as if we would be lost, raft and all. The water sucked our raft down until we were entirely under its surface, but we held on tightly, and after a seemingly interminable time, the craft steadied itself and arose slowly to the surface. We finally escaped its clutches and floated past, gasping for breath, but glad to be alive.

While we were arranging our camp on the second day, the canoes of the exploring party we had left up the river came into view. As the party passed, our friends called out for us to follow, saying there was a *puesto* a short distance around the first bend of the river where they would camp. But we had become comfortably located and decided to remain where we were. The members of the expedition had left Santa Rosa in the forenoon and had made this distance in seven hours. We had been two days on the journey, following the current as it wound around the longer edge of the turns, floating lazily along at times and at others whirling about in treacherous crosscurrents.

The mosquitoes, which had not been troublesome up to this time, attacked us with great persistence during the night, and we spent much of the time fighting them off. We had hoped to reach Cumaria, where netting could be purchased, before the insects became painfully attentive, but in this we were doomed to disappointment. Not only were we troubled by mosquitoes from this time on but were also greatly annoyed by the *manta blanca,* small insects that followed us all through the day, stinging whenever we paused in our efforts to fight them off.[8] It was not until now that we fully appreciated the attractiveness of the snow-capped Andes.

Despite our other troubles, however, one danger had been removed. There was no likelihood of our starving. Game was now plentiful and, what was more to the point, could be reached with greater ease. The nigritte herons, which were much in evidence, flapped laboriously from sandbar to sandbar. They manifested the most surprising curiosity, without taking flight until we were almost upon them. The garza rosada, or pink spoonbill, evinced more timidity, rising with a flurry upon our approach—a clumsy bunch of wildly agitated pink.[9]

We became so absorbed in watching the movements of these birds that we grew careless and paid the usual penalty of those who fail to exercise eternal vigilance upon this stream. Above the mouth of Río Curahuanta,[10] we were caught in a crosscurrent and dashed broadside against a barely submerged tree trunk, but we clung to and managed to get astride the raft, which was standing edgewise against the trunk, held there by the force of the current. We sat astride our queer steed, awaiting developments, because there was nothing else to be done. We could not hope to swim the rapids, and there seemed little hope of getting out in safety unless by chance someone should come to our rescue. The fates were kind in this instance, for the accident was seen by several women and children at a nearby settlement on the west bank. Owing to the excitement of the moment, they had escaped our notice. We could see them now as they ran about calling to one another, evidently making some preparation to come to our relief. While we watched them, the raft suddenly righted itself, and both Orton and I were thrown into the water, our grip upon the raft lost by the violence with which the craft was turned by the current. When I finally came to the surface, it was to see the raft about twenty feet to the right and Orton pulling himself aboard. I struck out as swiftly as possible and in a minute or two was clambering upon the bottom of the raft. It had turned completely over.

We were now in a very perilous position. Our paddles had floated away, and we were at the mercy of the stream. Moreover, all of our belongings were in our bags strapped on the underside of the raft, where it was absolutely impossible to reach them. While we gazed helplessly and hopelessly at one another, we noted two canoes coming in quick pursuit, manned by strong-limbed Indians. They soon overtook us, towed us ashore and helped us to right the raft. Marvelous luck! Our guns and bags were intact, and a portion of the food supply from Santa Rosa remained fast to the raft.

Though the accident occurred before the noon hour, our deliverers insisted on our remaining overnight, saying that we needed temporary relaxation from the dangers of the river. We accepted the invitation and spent a comfortable afternoon and night with our rescuer, Señor Sanchez. From his house, there was an excellent view of the river, and for the first time we fully appreciated the narrowness of our escape. About half a mile below where we were towed ashore, the river ran with tremendous force between narrow banks, great snags rearing up at frequent intervals. Had we been swept into the pass without any means of controlling the raft, we would have gone to almost certain destruction.

Following the recovery of our overturned raft, all went well for two days. At about nine o'clock on the morning of August 23, after an unusually long stretch of calm and sluggish water, we entered She-baya Pass.[11] The pass, a long, narrow race of swift crosscurrents, was thickly dotted with partially submerged trees, deposited by the sub-siding flood of the rainy season. These dangerous obstructions were so thick that from the moment we entered the pass it was necessary to bend every energy to avoid coming in contact with them. By dodg-ing from side to side of the onrushing current, we succeeded in getting almost through before disaster overtook us. The last obstruction in the pass was before us, and we could not avoid it. Just as it seemed that we would get by in safety, a crosscurrent caught the raft and dashed it violently to one side. It struck with great force against the partially submerged tree trunk, and the force of collision tore the raft to pieces. Catapulted into the seething water, I sank, but came to the surface in a moment, gripped one of the logs torn from the raft and was carried rapidly along. Looking back, I saw Orton clinging to the tree trunk that had wrecked us. He was holding on with his hands, his feet and body stretched toward me as the swift current tugged vi-ciously to break his hold. I cried as loud as I could, "Turn loose and swim to me! Turn loose and swim to me!" But he made no effort to reach me, and I cried out again, "Climb on the snag and wait. I'll come for you. Climb up! Climb up!" If he answered, I did not hear and, a few moments later, was borne beyond the range of vision.

After drifting a short time, holding to the log and attempting with one hand to direct it shoreward, I saw two Indians poling upstream in a canoe. By shouting repeatedly, I attracted their attention, and they started toward me. I called to them in Spanish as loud as I could, "Go in the pass. Go up the pass. My companion is on a snag!" I finally made them understand, and they proceeded upstream as rapidly as possible.

By this time the current had carried me near the left bank, and, by using my hands as oars, I succeeded in working my way close enough to shore to cast the log adrift and swim to safety. Immediately I directed my attention to the pass and saw the canoe enter, advance to a point above the snag and then come back. The Indians worked their way about the snag, evidently looking all around it, and then came back to where I had landed. One of the Indians, who could speak Spanish, informed me that no trace of my companion could be found. While he explained, another Indian, accompanied by his family, came through the pass, and I hailed him when he approached. When questioned, he said that he certainly would have seen anyone on or about the snag, as he passed close to it.

Thus James Orton, a native of Manchester, England, met his death. I saw him last as he clung to the snag, there in the midst of the swirling waters.

Finally realizing the utter hopelessness of the situation, I persuaded the Indians to row me to Cumaria. As we shoved out into the stream and were caught by the swift-moving current, I felt keenly the utter isolation of my position and the loss I had sustained. For so many months, Orton and I had been together constantly. We had braved perils and shared hardships. I had become greatly attached to him, won both by his splendid courage and his kindly qualities as a man, and when I realized that he was no more, that henceforth the perils and hardships of the voyage must be borne without his companionship, tears welled in my eyes and mingled with the waters that had become his grave.

In the wreck of the craft I lost everything except the few belongings upon my body. Owing to the frequency with which Orton and I were drenched with water, and to be unhampered as much as possible, it was our custom to put our clothes in the waterproof bag during the day and wear as little as possible. Thus it happened that I had nothing on but a few torn garments when the wreck occurred. The six-shooter was the only weapon I saved from the wreck, due to the fact that it was strapped on. My passport, permits and other papers, together with some few valuables, were worn under my shirt in a small rubber bag, and these things escaped injury.

En route downstream, I learned that the French expedition was camped at Cumaria. We reached there about nightfall. Dressed in a torn sweater and ragged trousers, barefooted and hatless, I presented myself at the camp. My story briefly told, I was given a warm welcome and told to make myself at home as long as I wished. I slept for eighteen hours, relieved for the time being of the great tension under which I had labored. For days after my arrival, we watched the river for the body of Orton, thinking perhaps it might drift by. We also asked the Indians connected with the camp to keep a sharp lookout, but it was never seen.

The memory of the night Orton and I spent in that simple home only days before, within the sullen roars of the narrow pass, is deeply impressed upon my mind. It was the last time we sat down together in comfort beneath a friendly roof. Unknown to us, he stood upon the brink of eternity, unconscious of his fate. I recall him as he was that night, making light of the perils through which we had passed and looking with hope and joyous anticipation to the time when we would again enter the circle of civilization and mingle with our fellows. He had traveled the world over, enduring hardship in the pursuit of adventure, and was rich in the lore of experience. As a world traveler, he knew the value of the exploration we had made together, and he often spoke in a laughing way of the manner in which honors would be heaped upon him when he returned to dear old England. He loved the little island, and pride in his achievements was national rather than personal. He believed there was an element of glory in making such a journey as ours into the wilds of a vast and practically unknown territory, and he felt that it was a glory that could be shared by the country of his nativity. Orton had often spoken of Stanley,[12] of the renown he brought to his country and the honors he received there, and it was evident that he felt he, too, would aid in rendering service as had that great explorer.

Whenever we sat at ease with pipes aglow, his dissertations upon the future were half humorous and half serious. He pictured a splendid reception for us when our work was done. Then the smile would pass from his face and the jest from his lips as his thoughts turned to the old home across the sea. The English love of adventure had taken deep root in him, but not more so than the love of home and country so typical of that people. With his passing, England lost a sturdy son, a fitting representative of that bold type to whose courage and devotion the British standard has been planted in the remote corners of the world.

Having set his heart upon exploring that unknown forest, no thought of retreating ever entered his mind. He walked with kingly courage into its dark embrace, and there he sleeps today, the mad waters of the Alto Ucayali singing an endless requiem to his soul.

PART THREE

Cumaria to New York City

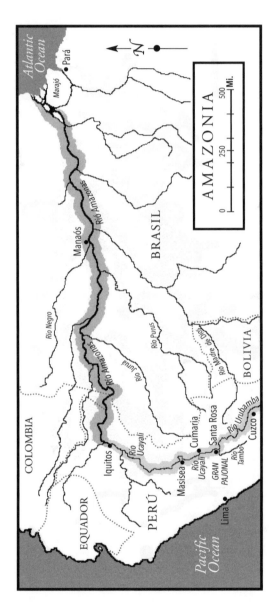

More than a thousand rivers and streams feed the Amazon River throughout its 4,345-mile course. Río Urubamba flows northwest 535 miles before merging with Río Tambo to form Río Ucayali, the Amazon's major tributary. The headwaters of the Urubamba are one of the most distant sources of the Amazon.

10

∿∿

CORPORATION OF SOME MAGNITUDE was financing the French expedition and had secured valuable concessions in this isolated quarter of Perú, and the engineers had been there for many months, mapping out prospective enterprises, and they were now awaiting the arrival of a relief party from Iquitos. At Cumaria, anticipation of this launch had become an absorbing theme. The rainy season was not far off, and the outgoing members of the expedition were anxious to get away before it began. Expecting to journey with them to Iquitos, I soon shared in the wait for the long overdue vessel.

I learned from the expedition that the boundary between Perú and Brasil, as defined by Brasilian maps, begins about 71° 30' W and 10° 30' S. On the Peruvian map, it begins about 72° W and 7° S. The two maps are official and, to say the least, confusing. Frequent disputes over these boundary markings are behind nine tenths of the war talk that so frequently furnishes more or less entertaining reading for the people in the States. The chief trouble seems to be that the headwaters of the streams forming the division lines are unknown. The result is that when a rich rubber section is discovered, each country seeks to locate it within its territory. The land being split up by almost innumerable streams, each country chooses the stream that gives it the most territory as the main branch of the river marking the boundary.[1]

Harrowing details of the conflict arising over the boundary question are told by rubber collectors. Following one dispute regarding the headwaters of the Purus River, vast quantities of rubber were destroyed to prevent their falling into the hands of the confiscating party. In a spirit of revenge, the invaders slew the heads of families, outraged the women and forced many of them into slavery. The desperate women are said to have placed poison in their conquerors' food. In that almost inaccessible region, might is right, and every man is a law unto himself. It is a subject of frequent comment that women persuaded into entering this region are forced into slavery and rarely ever reach the outer world again. It is a common practice for a rubber collector to take a half-caste girl into the forest with him as his wife. Later, when he is ready to return to market, she is sold, usually to another rubber collector. The forest knows its heartbreaking tragedies as truly as the outer world does.[2]

With affairs in a waiting state, we spent the days in the shadow of our huts. Nets were provided for protection against the mosquitoes and *manta blancas.* To wander outside the immediate vicinity of the camp was a painful experience. The grass was alive with very small red insects that attacked with great persistence, determined to taste the white man. It was necessary to sponge one's body each night with a weak solution of mercury to remove the day's accumulation of these insects. If not removed, they burrowed beneath the skin and caused painful irritations. The natives seemed unmindful of these insects as well as the mosquitoes. When not eating or sleeping, they whiled the hours away in a game of cards they called *truco,* the mysteries of which I did not attempt to solve.

The hum and drone of the insects and shrill notes of the paroquets as they circled about the trees were occasionally interrupted by the boisterous laughter of Conibo canoe boys who frolicked in the sun, ignoring the fierce intensity with which it streamed down upon their almost naked bodies. They smoked rank tobacco, cutting it into bits with small knives they carried attached to a string around the neck. Their pipes, made after a fashion all their own, were remarkable both in size and shape. The bowl, made of the small end of some animal's horn, was about six inches long, while the stem was barely long enough to grasp between the teeth. A hot smoke and a long one, but they seemed to enjoy it hugely.

At dusk on the nineteenth day after my arrival, every day having been spent in anxious waiting, an electric thrill went through the camp when the cry was raised: "The launch! The launch!" All eyes were directed down the river, and a cheer went up when a screw-propelled steamer of about forty tons was seen making its way upstream, just rounding a bend in the river about two hundred yards distant.

This boat, however, brought no news of the relief expedition. So it was decided that the American manager and five other members of the expedition should remain in charge of the Santa Rosa camp. The captain of the launch agreed to return this party up the river to Tahuanía,[3] from which point they could proceed by canoe to Santa Rosa and there await the relief corps in greater comfort. The manager invited me to join the expedition and remain with them until the reinforcements arrived. He was planning a trek from the camp at Santa Rosa into the unexplored Gran Pajonal, known to be inhabited by hostile tribes. Though consumed with anxiety to get safely away, I accepted. The prospect of this adventure compensated somewhat for the disappointment of not proceeding by launch to Iquitos and by ocean steamer down the Amazon.

Preparations for returning to Santa Rosa got under way with the manager, five other members of the expedition and myself aboard the launch, towing our canoes. On reaching Tahuanía, a half day's journey upriver, we found it impossible to hire Indians for poling and steering the canoes, so the manager and I decided to act as steersmen and leave our men to the punting.[4] Under ordinary circumstances, the Indian

129

is superior to the white man as a helmsman, having spent most of his life on the water, but when an upset seems probable, the white man is perhaps more likely to arise to the occasion. He can change his plans instantly, while the Indian hasn't this agility. When we started out, the captain of the launch seemed astonished to see white men steering canoes up the swift, treacherous stream. It was evident that he expected us to come to grief and blew the vessel's whistle in doleful farewell when he turned downstream for his return voyage to Iquitos.

Progress up the river was exceedingly difficult. We had to exercise the utmost caution to prevent capsizing and losing our cargo, and at a point where the river split into three streams, fully half a day was spent advancing one mile.

About noon on the ninth day after leaving Tahuanía, Santa Rosa came into view. It was in many respects an ideal camping place. The buildings had been constructed of palm wood, the most satisfactory and enduring material for that purpose to be found in the basin. Palm trunks planted deep in the ground supported the palm-thatched roof—a cover that lasts for years and deflects the heat of the sun as well as the heavy tropical rain. The floor was positioned some feet above the ground to afford ventilation and protection from the dampness of the earth during the rainy season. Split sections of the palm tree furnished boards for the walls and floors, and also for the light partitions that formed the rooms. Vines held the wood together since nails do not enter into the construction of houses in this part of the world. Because the houses built at this post differed somewhat from the prevailing style of architecture in the basin, the prediction was freely made that they would blow down during "the big wind," which according to local forecast always came on August 29. The blow had occurred on schedule, and the buildings withstood it.

11

OUR HOUSE IN ORDER, we began preparations for the expedition that had been planned pending the arrival of reinforcements. Led by the chief engineer, the party of ten would consist of four of the other expedition men, three Indians, a rubber collector (the owner of the Santa Rosa station) and myself. The territory we were to explore, which in all probability had never been invaded by a white man, stretched toward the west, a great sea of forest growth that swept across the distant chain of hills and became lost in the valleys beyond.

Following the Indian guide, we started for the distant hills, our route leading along an Indian trail that was nothing less than a tunnel through the forest. Only wide enough to allow single-file formation, the path was completely overgrown by tangled vines and overhanging limbs. So dense was the undergrowth that it was impossible to see more than ten feet to the right or left, while the growth overhead was so closely woven that only a suggestion of daylight trickled down from the small expanse above. In the early afternoon, we reached the summit of the first range of hills, and from this point we could see a second range lying some distance beyond. We decided to push on before resting for the night, but progress through the undergrowth was so slow that we barely reached the base of the second series of hills before twilight settled about us, so we hastily made camp.

While passing through the second valley, our guide informed us that he saw unmistakable evidence of the presence of hostile tribes and warned us against proceeding. We were not to be turned back so soon, but when we pitched camp for the night and sat about the fire, our ears assailed by the mysterious sounds of the forest, we gave due weight to the testimony of the guide. Our decision was to continue, even at the risk of a chance encounter with the savages, and at early dawn, the march toward the summit began. Near the backbone of the ridge, which was reached before noon, the Indians erected five snug little huts from palm leaves in less than an hour. The speed and skill with which they constructed these temporary shelters was always a source of wonder and admiration to me.

Investigation showed that a good view of the surrounding country could not be had at any point near this camp, and we decided to push on along a narrow ridge toward a higher elevation. Near the top of the ridge, we crossed a well-worn trail leading in the direction of the main river. It was once the great highway of the slave traffic between the Gran Pajonal and the Logoto slave station, followed by the conquering tribes when they disposed of their prisoners at the once famous post. Now it had fallen into disuse, the greater part of the slave traffic having been transferred to a station at the junction of the Unini River,[1] a day's journey by canoe below the mouth of the Tambo. This station is operated by a Spaniard, Vasada by name. From his post near the Unini River, expeditions are made by his Indians into the Gran Pajonal, where boys and girls are taken into captivity, their parents slain if resistance is offered. On one occasion I visited the camp of this animal and, much against my will, dined at his house. He was surrounded by hordes of retainers, whose loyalty was no doubt due in part to the fact that they were permitted to treat the captured Indian maidens as their fancy dictated—an example set by the Spaniard himself, as well as his numerous half-breed offspring.

When we reached this old trail, mute witness of man's inhumanity to man, the Indians were opposed to going farther. They said the Pajonal Indians were enemies of their tribe, spoke a different dialect and in all probability would misunderstand the purpose of our expedition. The result, they said, would be a night attack in which every member of our party would very likely be put to death. Questioned as to the location of the nearest known village of these hostile tribes, our Indians said it was about five days travel—for an Indian. They added that hunting parties were frequently seen in the neighborhood and expressed the conviction that such a party was at the moment sufficiently near enough to note the glow of our fires and learn the strength of our numbers.

Farther along the elevation, we discovered the unmistakable signs of a recent hunting excursion, but remained unwilling to turn back. However, we took the precaution to pitch our camp at a place protected by a sheer drop on three sides. Here we could easily have held our own against a large force of savages. This camp was also ideal from a scenic standpoint. In the morning, after a few trees that obstructed the view had been felled and the rays of the morning sun sent the mist scurrying from the valleys below, a scene of grandeur, such as is the privilege of few ever to behold, spread before us. Wrapped in the dreamy haze of distance, caressed by fleecy, changing clouds of filmy substance, the giant peaks of the Andes receded toward the Pacific. White flecked, these peaks seemed like mighty waves poised one above the other, each ready to sweep on and on into the distance, yet each as fixed as the sun that blazed above. Vast, somber and still, the valley below gave no answering echo to our exclamation of delight. The sleep of ages seemed to be upon it. No white man with noisy axe had ever disturbed its stillness. Untouched, unknown, it stretched its lazy length to the feet of the Andes, an empire given over to savages whose number is known to no man and whose very existence is known to comparatively few.

As we stood drinking in this scene, the sound of falling water came to us as if from a great distance, and, using field glasses, we discovered a stream apparently fifty feet in width and a sheer leap of some two hundred feet below the cliff. Determined to investigate it, I got the manager's consent to let the guide and one of the other Indians accompany me in an effort to reach it. After a descent of three hours, we reached the valley and then cut our way through the undergrowth. After two hours of slow progress, we arrived at the stream, but could get no view of the falls itself. At this point the Indians became stubborn and insisted on turning back. They said that to proceed meant spending the night there, separated from our party, and they were unwilling to run the risk. I was loath to give up, but it was undoubtedly the wisest thing to do, as it would have been dangerous to become separated.

The falls, examined critically through field glasses from the nearest point of view, appeared to flow from a great opening in the mountain and into the valley. It was a most remarkable formation with the appearance of a great hose being turned upon the valley; the opening, which seemed to be a hole, played the part of a nozzle. Later, the engineer placed this unique waterfall upon his map, naming it Williams Falls in recognition of my determined effort to reach and explore it.

That night he told me he had gained a splendid view of the country toward the southeast by means of climbing irons.[2] He had felled some trees on the ridge, and the country lying in between and beyond the main river was now in plain view. The following morning I climbed this tree and watched the sun dispel the mist that hung over the stream below, clearly marking its course. When the mist melted into nothingness, the stream's serpentine windings could be followed for miles. It appeared to mount upward and into the blue of the horizon. The mighty Ucayali, now many miles distant and fully 2,500 feet below, seemed like a silver thread as it wound through the forest, which swept in a level expanse toward the north and east. These waterways are the only highways of this territory, the invasion by the outside world having been confined to the immediate vicinity of the streams. What these lands really contain is largely a matter of speculation, and the information of the rubber collectors is superficial, applying only to a very limited territory. About all that is truly known of the great expanse upon which I gazed from the swaying treetops is that the Piro, Amahuaca and Shipibo tribes make their homes within its confines.[3]

The result of our exploration was a general idea of the topography of the country to the west. Although we felt keenly desirous of penetrating farther, the conditions were not favorable. Our Indian guide feared there might be a settlement of hostile tribesmen in the next valley, and the Indians were opposed to advancing. Generally, these settlements are protected by pits in which sharpened stakes are planted, so skillfully covered that the intruder is unaware that they exist until he is trapped. The fact was known to the Indians of our party, and they were not prepared to risk it. We turned back, but with the intent of again taking it up again if a Pajonal savage could be hired as our guide.

At the first camp on the return trail, one of the men on watch aroused us during the night when he heard people calling to one another in the forest. This created some alarm, but the Indians, after listening for a few moments to the cries now audible to all, relieved the situation by explaining that it was the call of the *tontaco*— a night bird.[4] It is the most human sound I have ever heard from either bird or beast, and anyone except an Indian would make our watchman's mistake. My first impression was that savages were about to attack, as it is their custom to attack just before dawn and to imitate the cry of the night bird in signaling to one another while surrounding the camp of their intended victims.

On this expedition, we had thought our guns would supply meat for the party, but game proved to be scarce, and once more I would be reduced to eating monkey. Search the forest as we would, monkeys were the only animals we could find, and their flesh became an unvarying diet. The monkeys, though plentiful, were remarkably alert and swift in their movements when alarmed, but could be tempted within range by a peculiar call sounded by the Indians. After being shot, it is not unusual for one of these animals to wind its tail around a limb and hang on for hours. When this occurred, an Indian had to climb the tree to get it. In the last three days of the trip, I finally overcame my prejudice against the flesh of the monkey. Up to that time I lived on rice and yuca meal, but our supply gave out, and it was eat monkey or go hungry.

When one of the Indian boys was bitten by a tarantula, the venom was extracted with a "snake stone." These stones are familiar possessions of the natives in all parts of the Indian country. Regarded as infallible, they are always used in pairs. When one is applied to the wound and it fails to adhere, the other is applied. It is claimed that one or the other always clings to the wound until the venom is absorbed. The expedition was equipped with hypodermic syringes and permanganate of potash for treating such wounds, but the Indians had great faith in the stones. In this case, it was thoroughly effective.[5]

After five days, we recrossed the Sapani River,[6] climbed the intervening mountain, traversed the tunnel of undergrowth and entered the Santa Rosa station, a tired, hungry and footsore crowd, the first white men who had ever ventured even a short distance into the Gran Pajonal country from the river.[7]

During our absence, no news had been received of the expected relief corps, and as soon as the novelty of the journey just taken had ceased to be an interesting topic of conversation, the monotony of our daily life began again. "How long will we be kept waiting?" This question bobbed up whenever conversation lagged.

12

∿∿∿

AYS GREW INTO WEEKS, and weeks stretched their weary lengths into months. Beginning in November with light but frequent showers, the rainy season was on in earnest by December. The whole earth was soggy with the superabundance of rain. Vegetation grew as if by magic with rank weeds climbing higher and multiplying by the hundreds. The murmur of the river increased to a roar, the crest of its murky flood ever striving for new levels, and the musty odor of sodden earth filled the air. At times the sun beat down fiercely, wringing clouds of steam from the reeking forest, but throughout most of the day the patter of the tropical downpour beat upon our ears. Time moved with feet that seemed never to have hurried since the world began, for there was nothing to do but wait—wait through the months of rain, wait for the mad river to spend its fury, wait for the succor that might come when this land of moods saw fit to smile again.

During this patience-trying period, we were forced to remain almost constantly indoors. The first month passed pleasantly, the American engineer and I whiling away the time by reading from our very limited supply of literature or in reciting our experiences, but the second became more wearisome and, after the succession of dull days, almost unbearable.

We arose at seven o'clock, and the morning bath was followed by coffee. Until eleven o'clock, we passed the time as best we could and then had breakfast. After that, an hour's siesta and then the weary wait until dinner, which was served at five o'clock. Three more monotonous hours, and to bed we went. This was the way we passed the days.

Since the dampness penetrated the utmost recesses of the building, all our apparel became sodden and mildewed unless kept in waterproof bags. Clothing, when washed, never thoroughly dried and soon became so weakened that a nominal strain caused an ominous r-r-rip. Boots and shoes required painstaking attention to preserve them for even a brief period of usefulness. Metal exposed for a single night became coated with rust, and to preserve our field instruments and weapons, we had to keep them coated with oil. Attacked by fever, ague and rheumatism, we were forced to consume quantities of gin and quinine in order to counteract their effect and preserve ourselves. Insects were beyond number, forcing us to remain within the protecting confines of a small netted area. Boots or shoes removed on retiring were always shaken carefully before being replaced, lest the ingress of the foot be disputed by a tarantula.

During the night a sudden shuffling on the floor indicated the presence of a snake running down a rat, a loathsome pest, which would have become extremely troublesome but for the fact that the snakes seemed perfectly willing to play the part of house cat after the occupants of the dwelling had retired. As all snakes in the region are considered venomous, a damp-proof case of matches was always kept convenient so that a light could be provided for examining the floor before trusting bare feet out of bed. Sometimes the sleeper was aroused by a wriggling beneath the cover, only to find that a harmless lizard had crept in to claim a share of the bed. Nightly, wild animals prowled about the place, snarling and growling in a manner to make us appreciate the height of the dwelling from the ground. Vampire bats beat against the netting, voicing with shrill cheep-cheep their desire to taste blood. The persistence of these bloodthirsty animals was such that dogs and even chickens had to be protected from their assaults. Our dog, a bull terrier, refused at first to sleep within the netted quarters, but was so reduced by their attacks that we confined him in a protected kennel.

One day, as I rummaged among our very limited store of books, I asked my companion, the engineer, "Where is Martin Chuzzlewit?"

"Oh, I don't know," he replied. "How many times lately have you read that book?"[1]

"Four times," I replied. "I'm trying to cultivate a jolly disposition while dwelling in this Eden."

"Fall into your hammock. I'll jolly you up with a yarn."

"Really," I replied, "I've… I've… just remembered that I want to do some writing."

"Come, be sociable."

"Well, if you're sure you haven't told it more than twice and I've not related it to you more than three times, I'll stand for it."

Many tales were told, told over and over again until each knew the other's stock as well as he knew it himself.

At length, Christmas Day 1907 arrived, a day of mist and dampness, of leaden sky and sweeping clouds. The patter upon the roof was not that of reindeer hoofs, for Santa Claus, if he knew that such a place as our camp existed, doubtless knew that there was no fireside and no mantel and no stocking to hang up. He doubtless also knew that there were no children in the camp, save the grownup children of misfortune.

Our thoughts naturally turned from the melancholy surroundings to brighter and happier scenes. With the drip of the rain above and drone of mosquitoes about me, I stretched at ease under my mosquito net and let memory wander far afield. Above the patter of the rain I seemed to hear the voice of sweet-toned bells in the village of my childhood, and, in fancy, could see the friends and loved ones of long ago wending their way to the modest temple of worship. I thought of the Christmas dinners of other years, and in meditating upon the friends and feasts of the past, I am sure that both my eyes and my mouth were made to water.[2] It was a dull day in our camp, and when the sun, as if weary of attempting to beat through the clouds, sank to rest, we were quick to follow the example, glad that the day so full of haunting memories had run its course.

The busy world can form but a dim conception of what Christmas means to those sturdy spirits who push their way into the remote places of the earth, suffering many ills, privations and hardships. These men, engineers as a rule, blaze the way for the march of progress, and it is a melancholy fact that they rarely taste the comforts and conveniences that follow by easy stages. As a rule, when developments have reached such a level that some of the pleasures of civilization become possible, duty calls them to other verdant fields, there to face anew the perils and hardships incident to their work. Bold frontiersmen, they are, always far in advance of the well ordered army of progress; builders, they are, whose monumental works are seen, but whose names are unknown and whose only glory is that of self accomplishment. Perhaps once or twice a year these engineers come in contact with their fellows and enjoy for a brief season the pleasant intercourse and creature comforts that to many people are commonplace, while the greater part of their lives is spent in isolated places, struggling to overcome for the world the obstacles that impede its advancement.

My companion was of this type. I recall that on Christmas Day, he said, "Only once in ten years have I spent Christmas in the outer world with friends and acquaintances." Then he spoke of the isolation of our position: "To the north and east lies a practically unknown region, a densely wooded wilderness, covering an area of a million square miles and embracing a large part of the forty thousand miles of navigable waterways in the Amazon basin. I venture the assertion that we are now in the most remote inhabited spot on the globe in point of accessibility and communication. One thousand miles north by river is Iquitos, our nearest post office. Santa Ana, is nearer by about three hundred miles, but the route up the river is, as you know, a more difficult and perilous journey."

"But the wireless telegraph station at Masisea[3] is only two hundred miles north of us," I interrupted.

"Yes, but it is practically impossible to reach it, and, moreover, it is unreliable. At times it seems to transmit satisfactorily, but occasions have been known when important communications were delayed a month. There is postal communication with the outer world at Iquitos and some probability of telegraphic communication at that point in the near future, but as matters stand now, the most accessible point of uninterrupted telegraphic communication is at Manaós, 3,500 miles distant."[4]

My companion continued, "For eleven years I have followed my calling throughout South America, the greater part of this time in almost inaccessible regions. Investigations have taken me from Panama to Tierra del Fuego. I have reported on properties of various kinds in northern, eastern and western Brasil, in southern and central Bolivia, in eastern Chile and in Ecuador. In the latter country I penetrated to a section where the natives were overcome with astonishment at the sight of a white man, their eyes never having beheld such a type. For months I have lived in Perú at elevations of 16,000 feet, up among the everlasting snowcaps and then suddenly changed my base of operations to a point more than three thousand miles distant, going up the Paraná River into the province of Mato Grosso,[5] where fever and beriberi are considered of mild importance even in the most favored sections. In making these changes, after months of isolation, I came occasionally in contact with cities and would enjoy a few days of pleasant intercourse with my fellows. Then it was on, on to the ragged edges of the world. Papers and periodicals six and eight months old have often contained information and news that was brand new to me."

The experience of this man is typical of many who are now engaged in extending the circle of civilization into the far reaches of the world.

The rainfall continued unabated until April. The total at our station for the five months, beginning in December, being 121 inches, a fraction over twenty-four inches a month.

13

ITH THE WANING of the rainy season, anxious eyes again turned down the river, eager for the first glimpse of the launch we felt would soon push its nose around the bend. The coming of the *Cuzco* was now the chief topic of conversation, interspersed with glowing details of what we would do when the long-expected vessel finally put in its appearance.

This wilderness existence had long since ceased to be a novel experience. The routine of daily life had grown to be a thing of present dread and painful anticipation. Thus the months of our exile dragged wearily along. The river had now been open to navigation for eight weeks, and the weather conditions were such that we could frequently take our after-meal smoke on the riverbank—always facing the bend. As we smoked, we pondered the whys and wherefores of the overdue boat and speculated upon the length of time we would be able to hold out under existing circumstances. With an ample supply of breadfruit, yuca root and bananas, and with plenty of game about, we were in no danger of starvation. However, our stock of sugar, coffee, tea and other luxuries had long been exhausted, and the store of medicine had vanished.

Another element added to the difficulties of the situation was the fact that the men had become dissatisfied with the long delay. It was practically impossible to find sufficient employment to keep them busy, and idleness proved a prolific breeder of discontent. Having much time to brood over their own affairs, they found themselves suffering from various ills, and these were magnified to an alarming extent at times. One day, a half-breed peón who had been assigned to cut some cedar paddles came in, explaining that he was suffering greatly from exposure to a poisonous tree. One of the evidences of this poison is a decided swelling of the affected member. This fellow explained that his face troubled him and insisted that he could not work. No evidence of the poison could be seen, and he was told to resume work. He became so vehement in his claim that he was suffering that the manager seized a mirror and handed it to him so that he could see there was an utter absence of swelling. The moment the peón gazed into the glass, he dropped it with a shriek, exclaiming, "*Maria Madre Dias!* The patrón says my face is not swollen, but I shall die before night." Inadvertently a mirror had been given to him with the magnifying side up, and in it, his face looked about four times its actual size. He was not poisoned, but he came near dying from fright.

During these weary days of waiting, the monotony of camp life was broken by the arrival of a Frenchman traveling by canoe to the Madre de Dios district. He was attended only by a Conibo Indian and was without the slightest knowledge of the dialect spoken by his guide. Although direct from Iquitos, the Frenchman brought but two items of news from the outside world. In frightfully disjointed Spanish he said that color photography had been discovered by a Frenchman and that the United States had dispatched a fleet of battleships to the Pacific.[1] Upon hearing that the United States fleet had sailed, a local *cauchero* [rubber gatherer] who had visited Iquitos on one or two occasions exclaimed, "*Caramba!*[2] To be in Iquitos! What a magnificent fiesta; a grand occasion; one occasion magnificent!"

"Why, what's the attraction in Iquitos?" I asked.

"Will not the armada visit Iquitos? Surely, yes, señor. Once a warship *Norte Americano* visited Iquitos, but I had not the honor to be there."

"I am ignorant of the intended ports of call," I said, "but I think it unlikely that even Pará will be visited by the squadron. Moreover, the Brasilians might object to the armada passing through their territory to reach Iquitos."[3]

"*Caramba,* señor, you do not know? The commandant of *Norte Americano,* when he was informed that a special permit was necessary to proceed to Iquitos, told the Brazzies that he regretted the seeming discourtesy, but 'will you, *excelentisimo, ilustrísimo,* honorable doctor senior official, kindly obtain the permit and have it ready upon my return?' and he steamed on. *Caramba,* I adore that *commandante.* Ever will he live in the memory of the Peruvians of the Loreto."

Iquitos, being the principal town in Perú east of the *cordilleras,*[4] is regarded with awe and veneration by this *cauchero.* He looks upon it as any rural youth in the United States is wont to regard the city of New York. Being the head of navigation for the lighter-draft, ocean-going vessels, it is the center of the rubber trade of Perú.[5] The rubber, as it comes directly from the forest, is carried to Iquitos by means of canoes and light-draft launches, and there transferred from the warehouses of the agents to the larger ships for worldwide distribution. Though fever-stricken at times and as yet without a hospital, Iquitos presents to the *cauchero* all of the color and life and gaiety that the outer world contains. While he toils and suffers in the swamps month after month, it is always with the picture of gay Iquitos before him, and while he labors, he dreams of the joys to come when the long season ends and he finds himself again in the whirl and excitement of this great world center. Once his rubber is disposed of, red wine will flow with a lavish disregard of consequences, financial or otherwise. In company with others of his kind, both male and female, he will make merry. This will continue day and night until his money is exhausted. Then, when he has sobered up sufficiently, he will seek out some local firm, enter into an agreement for supplies sufficient to meet his needs for the next two years and turn his face again towards the wilderness. Poling his laden canoe up the river for many days, he will finally select a suitable site and begin again the collection of rubber. The battle against the dangers of the jungles goes on as before, and when it is all over and he returns to Iquitos, it is to repeat the same performance. Two years of toil and two months of jag. This is about the sum total of his existence.

Caucheros are a great source of wealth for the Iquitos traders. They are honest as a rule and pay an enormous rate of interest when debts are contracted. Twenty percent is the average rate, whether the sum be for a month or a year. If they bought only to supply actual needs, they would prove poor pickings to the enterprising dealers, but they have an abnormal liking for gewgaws of all kinds. The forest supplies practically all their food, and they have little use for clothes. Tapirs, monkeys, wild hogs and birds abound, and they have a way all their own of catching fish in unlimited quantities. The barbasco plant, whose remarkable properties are well known to all the Indians, has the effect of stupefying every member of the finny tribe in the vicinity. The roots are pounded to a pulp and the mass is placed in a shallow part of the stream where the water runs swiftly. It is then kneaded underfoot for a time and soon the water for some distance below changes to a milky hue. The fish begin to leap about wildly in an effort to escape the drug, but in a short time they are overcome and float to the surface, belly up. As many fish as are wanted are gathered. As soon as the water clears, the fish remaining in the stream revive and seem to be no worse for the experience. This root will retain full strength for weeks if buried in the ground and will lose only about fifty percent of its efficiency when dried and left exposed to the atmosphere for several months. The plant exhausts a very unpleasant odor when being reduced to a pulp, but the Indians seem to be unmindful of the stench. Animals drinking stagnant water that has been polluted with it show immediate symptoms and almost invariably succumb after a prolonged sickness.[6]

With the departure of the Frenchman on his long and lonely journey, life in our camp dropped back into the old monotonous groove, and speculation turned once more upon the arrival of the launch. All through the waking hours, our eyes unconsciously sought the bend in the river, and at last our vigil was rewarded.

"The launch! The launch!"

This glad cry echoed through the camp one morning, and instantly there was a scene of bustle and preparation. About a mile distant a small launch had poked its nose around the bend and was now engaged in fighting its way against the onrushing current. A great shout went up, and I am not sure but that I expected some sort of a dance as an outward manifestation of inward glee. The tension relaxed at last, we became hysterical, and conversation was more by sign than by spoken word. Only those who have suffered long months of hardship, isolation, loneliness and uncertainty can appreciate the feeling that welled up in our hearts and found expression in quivering voice.

Though certain that it was the *Cuzco,* we attempted to make assurance double sure by leveling the field glasses to read the name on the launch. This was not possible, but presently a jet of steam arose, and we knew the boat was about to signal, and the signal would, according to the river code, establish its identity. A death-like silence fell upon us as we awaited the sound. Then it came: three long blasts followed by one so short that it seemed to have been choked off abruptly. "The *Cuzco,*" we exclaimed, and visions of newspapers and letters, as well as many material comforts, floated before us.

The vessel crept into the eddy waters at a *cauchero's* landing about three-quarters of a mile below and made fast. Some said, "Let's go down by canoe," but others said, "No, she is only stopping for wood and will come on before long." After what seemed an unnecessarily long stop, the little launch got under way again and resumed the battle with the current. Progress was painfully slow, and we wondered more than once if the boat would ever be able to stem the tide. When, almost within hailing distance of our camp, the launch suddenly turned its nose toward the opposite bank of the river. Instantly the cry went up: "She's not going to stop."

"Oh, yes, she will; she's only going over to escape the force of the current" was the reply of the more sanguine. Slowly, laboriously, the little craft fought its way across the rushing stream. Upon reaching quieter water, it rushed forward with a sudden burst of speed, and our hearts turned sick. Without a sign of recognition, it disappeared around an island pass a short distance above our camp. Dumb despair tugged at our hearts as we realized that all the glad hopes of an hour before were like the cinders that floated on the water in the little craft's wake. "Will the *Cuzco* come this year?" Not one among us had the courage at that moment to say it would.

A canoe was dispatched to the *cauchero's* landing, and there it was learned that the entire cargo of the vessel—the *Ucayali,* not the *Cuzco*—was consigned to the Madre de Dios district. A package had been left for the manager of our expedition, however. This was opened with eager curiosity, and a second disappointment awaited us when it was discovered that it contained nothing but a quantity of golden sovereigns sent from Iquitos by the financial agent of the expedition. Money, the most useless thing on earth at this moment.

14

⋀⋀

NEARLY A MONTH of waiting brought another launch
around the river bend, and this proved to be the *Cuzco,*
the long-expected launch that was to bring the relief
we had looked forward to for so many, many months.
But it brought disappointment, almost as keen as we had felt when
the *Ucayali* steamed by without a sign of recognition. The *Cuzco* was
bound upriver to Sepahua and left us with only a few unimportant
pieces of mail. Not a line of explanation, not a word of information
of the expected relief expedition. The manager was at his wits' end.
For nearly a year he had waited for fresh supplies and additional men,
and now that the rainy season had closed and the river would soon
recede to a point where navigation this far would be impossible, he
realized that reinforcements must come in a very short time or would
not arrive until another long period of rain, isolation and privation
had run its almost year-long course. He was tempted to quit the post
at once, but as the equipment in the camp was valued at many thousands of dollars, he was reluctant to leave it behind. He finally decided
to wait the limit, but made up his mind not to remain through
another rainy season.

The *Cuzco* carried one of the most unexpected of visitors, a
young physician on his annual trip up the river. He stopped at our

camp because the accommodations on the launch, owing to its crowded condition, were uncomfortable.

Within a month the *Cuzco* returned and tied up downstream at the *cauchero's* landing for another supply of wood. The captain, now very ill, sent a messenger by canoe requesting that the man of medicine come and treat him. But the doctor, fearing the canoe on our drift-bestrewn highway, suggested the launch come to our port. On the following morning the launch arrived quite early, so early that the doctor had not yet finished his morning nap. When aroused, he sent word to the captain to exercise patience; he would be "ready to receive" as soon as he had enjoyed his morning coffee and otherwise prepared for the day.

The axiom "pride goeth before a fall" holds good even on this river, as was shown a few days later with the arrival of the launch on which our medical friend expected to return to Iquitos. When it docked at the *cauchero's* landing, the doctor sent word by an Indian that he wished to take passage in exchange for the usual number of golden sovereigns. He received the desired permission, but was informed that he would have to proceed by canoe to the *cauchero's* landing or attempt to get aboard amid-stream opposite our camp.

Our stream, the only highway to civilization, was very busy on this particular day, so busy in moving the accumulation of driftwood and industriously forming whirlpools that the physician chose what he thought was the lesser of two dangers—to board the launch midstream. When the vessel came up to a point opposite our camp and paused in midstream, the doctor, accompanied by about thirty pieces of baggage, put off in a canoe. He reached the side of the launch in safety and was about to place his hands on its guardrail when the canoe and launch came together with a sudden bump and the canoe shipped a wave[1] that carried it over on its side. The deckhands hastily pulled the doctor aboard the launch, and a moment later the canoe capsized. From the deck, the bedraggled and disgusted young physician watched our canoe and his belongings float off down the stream, bobbing up and dancing around on the bosom of the river like bits of toast in an ocean of mud-colored soup. Then began a chase as laughable to us as it was exasperating to the doctor and the commander of the boat. The launch turned downstream in pursuit of the canoe and baggage. The elusive baggage and capsized canoe took kindly to every swift current and whirlpool. Ten minutes should have sufficed for the launch to land and take the physician aboard at our port; five hours' delay was the penalty paid for trifling with our highway.

The few exciting events of our existence now came in quick succession. Following the arrival of the launches and the visit of the physician, the cry of *"Tigre! Tigre!"* was heard in our camp one morning, the alarm having been raised by some Indian women and children about fifty yards distant. Seizing a rifle, I went forward to investigate. The women and children were congregated on the riverbank and seemed greatly excited. When I reached them, they pointed to a sandbar below and exclaimed, "There, there, señor, three *tigres!*" This was decidedly interesting. From where I stood I could see the footprints made by three jaguars, where they had landed upon the bar after swimming the river, and I hurried around to head them off before they would have to cross in making their way back into the forest depths. Turning a sharp bend in the trail I came face to face with a half-grown jaguar. I am at a loss to determine which was more surprised, the animal or I. I stopped stock still, and the jaguar did likewise. My rifle, presented right-handed, spoke. The shot was fired at such close range that it fully expected the jaguar to politely turn its toes skyward. Discourteous creature, he did nothing of the kind; sniffing his singed whiskers in evident surprise, he turned tail and fled. When I recalled hearing the yap, yap of the mother but a minute before I met the cub, I did not regret my clean miss. Had I wounded the cub, its cries would have brought me a fight for life.

A few days after this incident, I went into the forest to get some raw gum from a rubber tree with which to mend a rent in our clothes bag. Suddenly a tawny form flashed across the trail, and the crack of my rifle, fired from a hip position, was followed by a frantic threshing among the bushes. About ten feet from the trail, at the bottom of a shallow ditch, I found what was probably the mother of the invading trio of jaguars. The ball from my rifle had broken her spine, and she was dragging her body about by the forequarters. With fierce growls of pain and rage, she made vain but desperate efforts to spring upon my Indian attendant and me when we came into view. Another shot, and death followed a series of convulsive struggles. We paused only long enough to take her length with a piece of vine, as her flesh was unfit for human consumption and the skin was of no use to us. From nose to tip of tail, the length was five feet, six inches.

Time dragged along, each day bringing us nearer the hour when we must decide to give up all hope of relief and take our chances on getting back to civilization. The navigation season had closed at our port, though the river was still open to launches to a point about a week's journey by canoe below Santa Rosa. In a few more days, the head of navigation would drop many miles farther downstream.

On the Fourth of July, after about ten months of waiting, the manager of the expedition very reluctantly decided to abandon our camp. Taking only such articles as were necessary and could easily be carried in the canoe, we began our journey downstream, leaving the camp and its expensive equipment in the care of a rubber collector. The manager, our cook and I made the journey, our four peóns and other members of the expedition remaining at camp to try their luck as rubber gatherers.

The journey downstream was made without incident, and when we reached the head of navigation, we had the great good luck of finding a launch on the eve of its return to Iquitos. We arranged for passage and were soon on our way to the outer world—a long journey, it is true, but the change from the monotony of waiting to the certainty of travel was gratifying. The sensation of escaping was so exhilarating that the discomforts incidental to travel on one of these ill-equipped little steamers were momentarily forgotten.

Passengers on these little riverboats are placed in the same category with snags, crosscurrents and other hindrances along the river. The fare is so much per day, payable in gold, and the fixed charge must be met; it matters not how much time is spent in making the journey. The launches have no cabin accommodations; the passengers simply hang their hammocks on the deck and make themselves as comfortable as possible. Hammock hooks are placed four deep, and when the boat is crowded, the passengers sleep four deep—provided they sleep at all. Traveling with all deliberation and indifference to time, the launch frequently tied up at the port of some *cauchero* or other, and this was generally the signal for a dance tendered by the captain for the collector and his friends. These dances were always held on board, and they always meant sleepless nights. The deck space ordinarily given over to the hammocks was turned over to the dancers, and the passengers could either dance or make themselves as comfortable as possible upon a narrow rail that skirted the little vessel. We spent many sleepless nights fighting mosquitoes while the shore visitors made merry. The dances, which consumed so much time and caused so much inconvenience, are considered a necessary preliminary for opening negotiations for the purchase of rubber.

Fresh meat is rarely seen on board these launches; fish and turtle are the staple articles of diet. From constant practice, the people on these boats become so expert at eating fish that no attempt is made to remove the bones until the fish is placed in the mouth. Then the tongue seems to act as a separator, and the bones appear with astonishing rapidity. I gave offense to a native passenger on the boat by gazing thoroughly absorbed as the bones piled higher and higher on his plate. Voicing his annoyance, he said, "Have you never seen anyone eat fish before?"

"No, señor," I meekly replied.

FROM IQUITOS, the voyage down the Amazon on the steamship *Huayna* was so comfortable that it stood out in glaring contrast against the trip by launch from the wilderness, yet it was not without its tragic element.[2] Three cases of beriberi broke out on board during the journey, and one proved fatal, the victim a warrant officer in the Brasilian navy.[3] Upon his death, the ship paused in midstream while brawny British jack-tars went ashore and did what the denizens of the Brasilian settlement refused to do—toiled in the scorching tropical sun so a grave might be provided for the departed officer.

The unbounded region of green growth embracing the river on either side for thousands of miles offered an endless subject of speculation.[4] It is astonishing how little is known of this vast region. Travel in the interior is slow and tedious at best, and few care to venture beyond the well-beaten trail. A graphic idea of the great distances and the difficulties attending travel can be gathered from an incident in Brasil. In an attempt to quell a rebellion in Mato Grosso, a western province of the country, it was necessary to send a troop ship from Río de Janeiro up the Platte and Paraguay rivers, a distance of 1,900 miles by sea and 3,000 miles by river, to reach the seat of trouble. This undertaking consumed so much time that the rebel forces, after weeks of fighting, had won out and established a government of their own long before the reinforcements arrived on the scene.

The Amazon had grown in width from two miles at Iquitos to six miles at the port city of Manaós, Brasil.[5] This was the first cable station the *Huayna* reached, and my friend, the American manager of the defunct French expedition, took leave there for the purpose of communicating with the officials of his company while I continued on.

The river grew wider still until, at its mouth, this distance measured more than one hundred miles. I had then traveled, by my estimation, a total of 6,886 miles, roughly 4,800 of which covered the distance from the eastern headwaters to the mouth of this long and winding stream. At Pará,[6] on August 10, 1908, I disembarked from the *Huayna,* which was bound direct to Liverpool, and after a short delay took passage for New York on the SS *Cuthbert.*[7] Joy mixed with regret—regret that Orton, the brave and loyal companion who had shared the dangers of the journey with me, had not been spared to share the anticipation of this moment.

TWO MONTHS after leaving the heart of the wilderness, as I stood among the throngs on the Great White Way in New York City, it seemed that the rugged banks of Alto Amazon had by some strange magic become towering buildings, while the swirling waters were transformed into a restless tide of humanity. Great and wonderful the change, and keen my joy to behold it.

CONTRARY TO THE POPULAR IMPRESSION among South American visitors, who touch only at the port cities, the native of North America is the least liked of all foreigners in the Latin American countries. The air of condescending patronage that generally characterizes these visitors is intolerable to the native. In the interior, this feeling of dislike for the man from the States is more noticeable than on the coast, and it is very evident that if the closer relationship so often spoken of is ever to materialize, the people of North America will have to cease sneering at the "little republics," and the North American press will have to blue-pencil its outbursts of alleged humor with reference to "parlor rifle rebellions."

The Latin American people are extremely sensitive, and, as a rule, the members of the upper class are highly educated. They take their country, their wars and their history seriously, and in pride of home and patriotism, yield first place to no nation under heaven. Their knowledge of the nonchalant North American is far more accurate than the latter's knowledge of them. Many of their sons and daughters are educated in the higher institutions of the United States and have gone on absorbing information about the great country to the north, while people there have paid little or no attention to the people south of them.

The resources of South America have merely been scratched, as the expression goes. Countless millions are to be made there, and if the manufacturers, financiers and other businessmen of the United States are to share in the ever-increasing yield, it is time they undertook, earnestly and seriously, the work of reconciling differences, removing unfavorable impressions and promoting understanding and a real friendship, instead of the misunderstandings and fictitious friendships of today.

Lee English Williams

LEE ENGLISH WILLIAMS described himself as a "man to whom change is mistress and chance counselor." To the editors of the *New Orleans Times-Democrat*, he was a "modest Southern sailor boy."

Reconstruction in the deep South was long under way when Williams was born near Munford in Talladega County, Alabama, in 1875. He was named for Robert E. Lee, under whom his father, Thomas Williams, had served at Gettysburg, as well as for the family of his mother, Laura English. His grandparents had been among the pioneer settlers drawn to east Alabama in 1834 when the General Land Office began selling the former Creek Indian lands there. Thomas was from a family of schoolteachers and preachers; Laura, from a respectable farming family.

Thomas, having no interest in farming, followed his two older brothers to Selma in southwest Alabama, where he went to work in the office of a cotton processing business. Laura and their six children summered with her widowed mother in the countryside, where Lee, the eldest, found adventure in roaming the woods and creeks that surrounded the English family's cotton fields. In Selma, he attended the college preparatory school for young men founded by one of his uncles. It provided an education that opened his eyes to the outside world: "When as a young boy I played around the farm of my maternal grandmother, if the prediction had been made that I would be a world-wide wanderer, the very suggestion would have met with vehement denial." Upon graduating in 1893, he became a seaman. Eight years of wandering led him to South Africa, where he joined the horde of foreigners prospecting for gold. Whatever succcess he had was enough to finance his next move: to Buenos Aires, Argentina, in 1906.

Only a narrow paper trail of official documents reveals what became of Williams after the *Times-Democrat* published his memoir. He registered for the World War I draft in Lumberton, Mississippi, in 1918, stating that he was married and resided there, but employed as a machinist for DuPont Engineering in Jacksonville, Tennessee. Two years later, he was working as an insurance agent in Purvis, Mississippi. The childless marriage would end in divorce before he applied for a seaman's certificate of citizenship in New Orleans in 1925. This was the standard documentation required of crew members of U.S. ocean-going vessels. It freed him to travel the world as a merchant mariner. He was then fifty years old, although he stated his age as forty-one. Census records thereafter show him lodging in boarding houses that catered to seamen in Wilmington, Delaware, and Galveston, Texas, where in 1942 he voluntarily registered for the World War II draft. He was sixty-seven years old, but claimed to be sixty-one. The trail ends there.

In *Heart of Darkness,* Joseph Conrad describes men who "'followed the sea' with reverence and affection." Williams was surely of this sort. One can only imagine his final years, the old man among the crew of some merchant vessel, still following the sea. His possessions are few, the tattered pages from an old newspaper having been somewhere left behind, lost to time. But ask him for a story, and he'll scratch his memory for some moment from long ago, light his pipe and launch forth: "On the fifth day that we'd been without food, we landed at a point where a small stream flowed in from the forest..."

NOTES

With any work of nonfiction, fact-checking becomes the most essential and critical aspect of an editor's job. Williams was writing about a place and time that were largely unknown to me, and I made hundreds of notes as I read and reread his chapters. For the reader who may have questions or wish to know more, many of those notes that satisfied my fledgling curiosity are included on these pages.

Introduction

1. The title, *Far from the Beaten Track,* is a well-worn expression from the turn of the last century. It struck me as too offhand for this journey into one of the last unknown places on earth, and I replaced it with *Amazonia 1907.* The subtitle "Outside the Circle of Civilization" is from Williams's text and appears to be original.

2. As published in the *New Orleans Times-Democrat,* the chapters often end with a cliff-hanger, a device typical of serialized stories and intended to maintain the reader's interest from week to week. Revisions were made to resolve several of these situations before the end of the chapters in which they occur.

3. I was unable to learn anything more about Orton beyond what Williams states. Another James Orton, an American professor at Vassar College, led three geological expeditions to Perú, where he died in 1877. I had hoped there might be a connection, but it was pure coincidence.

4. In Williams's day, *wanderlust* was a relatively new word, having first appeared in print in Germany in 1902. It's a good word.

5. Paul Marcoy (born Laurent de Saint-Cricq) documented the French expedition in four self-illustrated volumes that were published in English as *Travels in South America, From the Pacific Ocean to the Atlantic Ocean* in 1873.

6. Peter Matthiessen's series of three articles about his travels in South America appeared in the *New Yorker* in 1961 prior to their publication by Viking Press as *The Cloud Forest: A Chronicle of the South American Wilderness.*

Chapter 1

1. The SS *Surrey* (Federal Steam Navigation Co. Ltd.) regularly sailed between London and Sydney, via Cape Town. J.G. Barrow, a British missionary who was among Williams's fellow passengers, wrote in a letter that the ship left Cape Town on April 1, 1906, and landed at the island of Tristan da Cunha on April 8.

2. The term *east and west of Suez* referred to Great Britain's interests outside the European theatre, specifically in the Middle East and Africa.

3. Tristan da Cunha is the largest in a group of volcanic islands in the south Atlantic Ocean. The most remote inhabited archipelago on earth, it lies 1,500 miles from South Africa and 2,000 miles from South America. It has been inhabited since 1810, and its population in recent years numbers about three hundred hardy souls.

4. *Jack-tar* is a British term for seamen, particularly of the merchant marine and Royal Navy.

5. J.G. Barrow, the missionary passenger, wrote: "This boat is taking the first mail from the Cape [to Tristan da Cunha] for two years." A postcard mailed from Tristan da Cunha by J. Rowley, another passenger, and sold at auction in 2012 was addressed to "R. Henderson Esq., General Post Office, Cape Town," and the return address was simply "SS Surrey, Is. of Tristan da Cunha, 1566 miles from C. Town." Rowley wrote: "This card may reach you before the end of next year. Treasure it! There is no Postal Administration here."

6. At the turn of the twentieth century, Montevideo, the Atlantic coastal capital of Uruguay, had a population that exceeded 300,000, one third of whom were foreign born.

7. Buenos Aires, which lies on the western shore of Río de la Plata estuary, about 175 miles by ship from Montevideo, is the capital of the Argentine Republic. In 1906, the city was as cosmopolitan as the European capitals, a steady stream of immigrants from Spain, Italy and Central Europe having swelled its population to nearly one million.

After three centuries as a Spanish colony, Argentina had declared its independence in 1816 as the Argentine Republic. (In the early twentieth century, it was referred to as "the Argentine" throughout the English-speaking world.) After political stability was achieved in 1880, Argentina began aggressively promoting emigration from Europe. Having reinvented itself, Argentina became the seventh wealthiest nation by 1908.

8. Rosario was then a modern city on the Paraná River, 185 miles north-west of Buenos Aires. Today, it is Argentina's third most populous city.

9. San Miguel de Tucumán, on the slopes of the Aconquija mountains 815 miles from Buenos Aires, was then the leading city in northern Argentina.

10. San Salvador de Jujuy, generally known as Jujuy, is the capital of the Jujuy Province, which borders Chile and Bolivia in the extreme northwest corner of Argentina. Its large aboriginal population sharply contrasted with the multicultural makeup of the country's larger cities to the south.

11. Maté is an herbal tea, originally served in a hollowed gourd and consumed through a hollow cane straw. It is said to have medicinal properties.

12. Quebrada de Humahuaca is a narrow mountain gorge with steep slopes; it extends 95 miles from north to south. During the winter months (June to August), it remains dry, but the Río Grande spills into it during the summer.

13. Known as *Carnaval* throughout Argentina, Mardi Gras marks the beginning of Lent.

14. This is a variation of *corrida de sortija,* a traditional gaucho sport.

15. The word *chicha* is generic for a wide variety of fermented beverages popular throughout Central and South America. *Chicha de jora,* a beer made from fermented corn, has been brewed and consumed in communities in the Andes for millennia. There are numerous methods for preparing it, aside from the one Williams describes.

16. Quechua is a family of Indian dialects spoken in the Andes and highlands of South America. Those who speak this language are generally referred to as Quechuas. Derived from the oral language of the Incas, who had no written language, Quechua remains, for the most part, a spoken language, although it's the source of many of the geographical place-names in a wide swath of territory extending from northern Argentina through Bolivia, Peru, Ecuador and Colombia.

17. "On with the dance! let joy be unconfin'd" is a line from Lord Byron's "Childe Harold's Pilgrimage." Mark Twain claimed it as his motto, with the disclaimer "…whether there's any dance to dance or joy to unconfine."

Chapter 2

1. Eighty miles north of Jujuy, Humahuaca is a town on the main road from Argentina into Bolivia. It overlooks the Río Grande and is surrounded by spectacularly colorful mountains. It has a long history as a staging point for expeditions to the Andes of Perú.

2. Tres Cruces, thirty miles beyond Humahuaca, is a village 14,800 ft. above sea level on the southern edge of the Altiplano, translated "high plateau." This plateau extends northward through western Bolivia and into southern Perú. Mostly barren, it is a relatively flat-floored depression about 500 miles long and 80 miles wide, at elevations around 12,000 feet. Aside from the Tibetan Plateau, the Altiplano is the most extensive area of high plateau on earth.

3. The landmark La Esquina Blanca is a large outcropping of limestone.

4. Abra Pampa is a mining town ten miles north of Tres Cruces. A *pampa*, derived from the Quechua language, is a flat, grass-covered plain.

5. The Spanish word *capilla* is translated "chapel." There is no town called Capilla on present-day maps.

6. A calabash is a vine gourd that, when dried and carved out, can serve as a vessel for liquids.

7. A mirage is a naturally occurring optical illusion that appears when certain atmospheric conditions cause light waves to bend and produce a displaced or inverted image of distant objects. The mirage Williams describes in such detail is highly unlikely, although some mirages are known to elevate objects that exist just beyond the distant horizon so they appear to be on the horizon.

8. La Quiaca was then a young town on the bank of Río La Quiaca, 180 miles from Jujuy and about 20 miles south of what was then Argentina's border with Bolivia. Today, the river forms the border between La Quiaca and its twin city Villazón in southern Bolivia.

9. In the mountainous regions of South America, the most reliable means of transporting produce and goods was by pack train: a line of burros, mules or llamas with loads in large bags slung over their backs.

10. Bolivia was part of the vast area conquered by Spain in the 16th century. It was known as Upper Perú until 1825, when, under the leadership of Simón Bolivar, it gained its independence. Over time, Bolivia surrendered its seacoast and much of its territory to its more powerful

neighboring countries, leaving it landlocked. Whatever prosperity it enjoyed in the 1800s came from the mining of silver, but by 1907, tin had become its most important product. The Bolivia that Williams traveled through was a predominantly rural nation, in which the majority Indian population was excluded by the Spanish-speaking minority. Having been forced for generations to work the mines, the uneducated Indians lived under the most primitive conditions.

The Andes mountains cover one-third of Bolivia. The area through which Williams journeyed—the Altiplano—lies between two mountain ranges extending from northern Argentina to southern Perú.

La Paz had become Bolivia's capital in 1898, nine years before Williams's arrival. Construction of railways linking La Paz to the Atlantic and Pacific coasts began in 1900. At 13,000 feet above sea level, La Paz has the highest elevation of any world capital.

11. Today, Mojo is a Bolivian town that serves no official function.

12. A boliviano, the currency of Bolivia, is comprised of 100 centavos. It was worth about forty cents in 1907.

13. A sovereign was a British gold coin worth one pound sterling that was used in international trade.

14. San Juan del Oro River, translated "St. John of Gold," is a stream south of Tupiza that remains dry much of the year. Nazaret (Spanish for "Nazareth") is not to be found on present-day maps.

15. Dramatic red rock canyons surround the town of Tupiza.

16. Charles Darwin called the *benchuca* "the great black bug of the Pampas," saying: "It is most disgusting to feel soft wingless insects, about an inch long, crawling over one's body; before sucking they are quite thin, but afterwards round and bloated with blood, and in this state they are easily squashed." Its bite can result in Chagas disease.

Chapter 3

1. Following the most direct route, the distance between Tupiza and Uyuni is 125 miles. Their route began on the northwest outskirts of Tupiza where they followed the Quebrada de Palala, a broad, deep ravine that becomes a tributary of the Tupiz River during the rainy season. A point of entry to the back country, it's lined with fantastic rock formations that rise like a forest of cathedral spires. From his years in Africa, Williams knew of Paul Kruger, one of the South African Republic's dominant political and military figures. Nicknamed Oom Paul (Uncle Paul),

he served as its president from 1883 to 1900.

2. Oro Ingenio (translated "gold ingenuity") appears on a 1931 map of Bolivia about 30 miles northwest of Tupiza. Thirty miles farther along the route they followed is San Vicente, where on November 6, 1908, Butch Cassidy and the Sundance Kid are said to have met their end, following a notorious series of armed robberies in Argentina and Bolivia.

3. A Basuto is a Basotho tribesman of southern South Africa.

4. *Tambos,* from the Quechua word *tampu* for an inn or way station, originated with the Incas. As they developed a system of roads, they constructed *tambos* along them, usually a day's journey apart. Some were little more than isolated shelters where traveling officials could spend a night, while others eventually became settlements. Other *tambos* are believed to have been large enough to house and feed an army.

5. A league is an approximate unit of measure that equates distance with time, one league being the distance an adult can walk in one hour, or roughly three miles on ordinary terrain.

6. Encoriani doesn't appear on early twentieth-century maps of Bolivia. Williams and his companions presumably slept that night at an inn. His description of the stone bed warmed by a fire beneath it cannot be confirmed, although another traveler of that time described an ordinary Bolivian home with "platforms of dried mud, which serve the purpose of bed and table."

7. This toxic plant was most likely a variety of Jimsonweed.

8. This was the *zorro de las pampas* (translated "plains fox").

9. Tambo Tambillo is an isolated village of mud-brick houses in the desert-like highlands of southwest Bolivia. Its one distinction is an enormous crater nearby that was created by a meteorite.

10. Uyuni is about 75 miles from Tambo Tambillo. At that time, Uyuni served as a distribution hub for trains hauling minerals to Pacific Ocean ports. The rail lines were built by British engineers, who formed a sizeable community in Uyuni. Ten miles northwest of the town is the edge of Salar de Uyuni, the world's largest salt plain. Covered by a solid crust of pure white salt, this immense, almost perfectly flat expanse covers nearly 4,000 square miles. Williams makes no mention of it.

11. Two hundred miles north of Uyuni, Oruro was established as a silver mining center. By the turn of the twentieth century, the silver deposits had been exhausted and Oruro's La Salvadoro mine was the world's leading source of tin. La Paz is 140 miles farther to the north.

12. The construction of railroads in landlocked Bolivia paralleled the development of that country's mining industry. Passenger service was by far secondary to the transport of ore. Initially, the rails ran westward to Chile's Pacific ports. British business interests took control of the entire system in 1903 and began expanding it into Perú and Argentina.

13. The peak of Kimsa Misa in the Bolivian Andes rises 15,700 ft. above sea level.

14. Viscachani is a mineral hot springs about 60 miles from La Paz.

15. The coca plant is native to western South America, where it has been cultivated and its leaves consumed for several thousand years. The chewed leaves not only produce a stimulating effect but are also rich in nutrients. To the Incas, coca was thought to be sacred, its use restricted to the upper echelon. Under Spain's rule, the indigenous laborers were encouraged to use coca in order to increase their stamina and tolerance for hunger and thirst.

In the mid 1800s, a market for the import of coca leaves developed in Europe and America. Numerous patent medicines, tonics and beverages were formulated from coca, most famously the original version of Coca-Cola in 1886. While chewed coca is considered nonaddictive, cocaine can be extracted from coca, which eventually resulted in coca becoming illegal in most countries outside South America.

16. At 21,200 feet, Illimani is the highest mountain in the Cordillera Real, a subrange of the Andes in western Bolivia.

The newly built railway from Lake Titicaca had reached El Alto in 1905. El Alto lies at the edge of a dry plain overlooking La Paz, seat of the Bolivian government, deep in the valley below. The La Paz rail yards, depot and housing for railway workers were constructed in El Alto, with a spur line descending to La Paz. Guaqui, sixty miles from La Paz, is the railhead and port on Lake Titicaca.

Chapter 4

1. Lake Titicaca lies on the border between Bolivia and Perú. It is the highest navigable lake in the world and, 138 miles in length and 69 miles wide, the largest in South America.

2. After nearly three centuries of Spanish domination, Perú won its independence in 1821, although political stability was only achieved in the 1890s. Lima, the capital city overlooking the Pacific Ocean, prospered most under the new elitist regime. Geographically, Perú has always been

two countries. Running parallel to the coastline, the mountains of the Andes separate the arid coast from eastern Perú and the country's bountiful natural resources—the Perú that Williams and Orton reached in April 1907. Cuzco is the primary eastern city and gateway to the Amazon basin, a vast tropical rain forest that drains into the Amazon River. In contrast with turn-of-the-century Lima, little had changed in Cuzco since Spanish colonial times.

The vitality of Perú's economy depended on exports, primarily fish from its coastal fisheries, minerals from its mountain mines and rubber from its tropical forests. In 1906, the government launched an international campaign for foreign investment in developing these industries. The mighty obstacle they faced was the lack of transportation from inland regions to Mollendo, Perú's Pacific seaport, and, more challenging, to the Atlantic via the Amazon River. This made road and railroad construction a priority.

3. Twenty-five miles north of Puno, Juliaca Junction was the first station of Ferrocarriles del Sur del Perú (Southern Railway). The tracks to Arequipa had been in service since 1876.

4. Arequipa, which then had a population of about 40,000, was strategically located as a link between the coastal and highland regions of southern Perú.

5. Construction of the Juliaca–Cuzco section of the Southern Railway had begun in 1872, but would not reach Cuzco until 1908. Sicuani is a small town, 120 miles from Juliaca and 90 miles from Cuzco. The "pinching valley" Williams mentions is La Raya Pass (Abra La Raya), the highest point on the rail route to Cuzco.

6. This "tiny stream" is Williams's first reference to the mighty Urubamba River, which is one of the "main headwaters" of the Amazon. Its source at La Raya Pass is a marsh created by a slowly melting glacier. From there it flows north more than 450 miles, ever increasing in volume, on a meandering course in the eastern shadow of the Andes. The Urubamba rushes past Inca ruins and Spanish colonial villages into the dense rain forest of the Amazon basin, from an altitude of 14,150 feet to 720 feet at which point it meets the Tambo River. Together, they form the Ucayali River, a major tributary of the Amazon.

To the Incas, the Urubamba was the sacred stream Willkamayu. Over the centuries of Spanish rule, segments of the river were locally known by names associated with the nearest important hacienda (Río de Sicuani,

Río de Calca and Río Santa Ana, to name a few), haciendas being large plantations. It was only in 1899 that the name Urubamba, from *Uru-pampa* in the Quechua language, was formalized, although some still refer to the upper Urubamba as Río Vilcanota.

Williams's confusion over the identity of what he sometimes refers to as "the main river" is understandable, especially to one encountering it on foot. On maps of his day, the location and course of this primary stream was at best approximate. Although the Urubamba flows in a northerly direction, it twists and turns toward every point on the compass, sometimes veering more than 300° over a short distance. Maps can hardly convey the complexity of its serpentine course.

7. Checacupe, a village on banks rising high above the Urubamba, has long been a crossing point, with a stone bridge from the Spanish colonial era leading to the church on the town square. There are no Inca temple ruins, only the reproduction of an Inca rope bridge to attract tourists.

8. What Williams calls a "traction train" was a lightweight locomotive that ran on the completed rails and was used for transporting supplies and workers to the construction site.

9. Located in southeastern Perú, Cuzco is the oldest continuously inhabited city in the Americas. It has been populated for more than 3,000 years and served as the imperial city of the Inca Empire from the 13th century until Spain's conquest in 1535, when Pizarro claimed the Inca lands for Spain and founded Lima 700 miles away on the Pacific coast as the colonial capital. The once magnificent Inca city was ignored after the Spanish conquest, mainly serving as a center for spreading Christianity to the Indians living in the isolated region.

When Williams and Orton arrived in 1907, Cuzco had a population of 30,000, but lacked electricity and other modern amenities. Spanish colonial buildings, many of them ecclesiastical, stood among the remains of Inca walls and atop the foundations of Inca temples and palaces. The American adventurer Harry Frank described turn-of-the-century Cusco as a "hotbed of [Catholic] fanaticism." The city's elevation, 11,200 ft. above sea level, accounts for the mostly barren surrounding landscape. Hiram Bingham, a South American scholar at Yale University wrote that Cuzco was "too high to have charming surroundings."

The Sacred Valley (Valle Sagrado de los Incas) is formed by the Urubamba River and stretches northwest of Cuzco to the Inca ruins at Machu Picchu, 45 miles away. In 1911, Bingham's rediscovery of Machu

Picchu excited interest in the Inca civilization and eventually made Cuzco an international destination for visitors.

10. A major public holiday in Perú, the feast of Corpus Christi occurs sixty days after Easter Sunday. In present-day Cuzco, this holiday continues to be celebrated just as Williams describes it: Processions of effigies representing fifteen saints and virgins converge on the cathedral at Plaza de Armas to "greet" the transformed body of Christ. Colorfully dressed crowds fill the streets and plaza, where dancers and musicians add to the festivity. In the evening, everyone enjoys a massive feast of traditional Andean dishes.

11. These would have been the ruins of Sacsayhuamán, once an imposing citadel on a steep hill on the northern outskirts of Cuzco. During the Spanish conquest, Pizarro's brother described it as built of "stones so large and thick that it seemed impossible that human hands could have set them in place.... They were so close together, and so well fitted, that the point of a pin could not have been inserted in one of the joints."

12. Pucyura is a village 15 miles northwest of Cuzco.

13. Huarocondo village lies about ten miles beyond Pucyura in an agricultural valley of rolling hills.

14. What Williams calls Olliante Fort and later Olliante Tambo is Ollantaytambo—second only to Machu Picchu among Perú's best preserved Inca sites. What remains are the Temple of the Sun and ranks of stone terraces on steep mountainsides with commanding views of the wide valley below. Constructed around the middle of the 15th century, Ollantaytambo served as a royal residence as well as a religious and administrative center. Williams assumed that mortar held the enormous stones in place, but the Incas cut and shaped them so precisely that they held firm without benefit of a cement. In fact, the walls have withstood time, the elements and numerous earthquakes, thanks to the absence of a mortar, which would have eventually crumbled and loosened the stones.

While the story of the Inca princess is most likely a romantic folktale, it refers to the Princess Bath, a surviving fountain carved from granite stones, that is believed to have originally served as a sacred bath for Inca sun virgins.

The function of Ollantaytambo's terraces had always been agricultural, not defensive as Williams suggests. It was not until Cuzco fell to Spain in 1533 that the Inca army retreated to Ollantaytambo and fortified its

approaches. As a fortress, it became the last stronghold of the Inca resistance. Ollanta, the town below, dates from the 15th century and is no-
table as the best surviving example of Inca city planning.

15. An alkali is a soluble salt obtained from the ashes of plants.

16. A water turbine for generating electricity, the Pelton wheel was invented in the 1870s. The concept proved so efficient that it remains in
production and use worldwide more than a century later.

One can only estimate the exact location of the unnamed officer's hacienda, certainly to the north of the ruins of Machu Picchu. In 1963 a
hydroelectric power plant was constructed on the Urubamba in a deep
gorge below Machu Picchu.

17. About twenty miles north of Machu Picchu, Santa Ana appears
prominently on maps of the area as early as 1834. It originated as a mission church in Spanish colonial days, when the valley first attracted settlers. The mission gave its name to the Santa Ana Valley, the large
Hacienda Santa Ana and even that portion of the Urubamba River that
passes through the valley. In the 1950s, Santa Ana became known as
Quillabamba, and the Santa Ana Valley as the Urubamba Valley.

In writing of his 1911 explorations, Hiram Bingham provides various
descriptions of Santa Ana and what he called the Urubamba Valley:
"Santa Ana is less than thirteen degrees south of the equator; the elevation
is barely 2,000 feet; the 'winter' nights are cool; but the heat in the middle
of the day is intense.... In the Urubamba Valley, there is everything to
please the eye and delight the horticulturalist.... Urubamba's gardens of
today are full of roses, lilies, and other brilliant flowers. There are orchards
of peaches, pears, and apples; there are fields where luscious strawberries
are raised for the Cuzco market.... The Urubamba River here meanders
through a broad, fertile valley, green with tropical plantations. We passed
groves of bananas and oranges, waving fields of green sugar cane, the
hospitable dwellings of prosperous planters, and the huts of Indians for-
tunate enough to dwell in this tropical 'Garden of Eden.'"

18. This was the Urubamba River.

19. Hacienda Santa Ana was a large plantation on the west side of Río
Urubamba overseen by Don Pedro Duque, who had married into the
Rueda family, the original owners of much of the valley. Isaiah Bowman,
a geographer with the Yale Peruvian Expedition of 1911, wrote, "There
is an interesting account of the settlement by the Rueda family of the
great estate still held by a Rueda, the wife of Señor Duque. José Rueda,

in 1829, was a government deputy representative and took his pay in land, acquiring valuable territory on which there was nothing more than a mission. In 1830 Rueda ceded certain lands in *arriendo* (rent) and on these were founded the haciendas Pucamoco, Sahuayaco, etc."

Four years after hosting Williams and Orton, Señor Duque extended the same hospitality to Hiram Bingham. His 1911 expedition financed by the Yale University and the National Geographic Society would make an archaeologist of him. In Cuzco, Bingham had become acquainted with Señor Duque's Notre Dame-educated son, Alberto, who lived on the plantation and, no doubt, extended an invitation to Bingham. In his writings, Bingham described the elder Duque: "Reputed to be the wisest and ablest man in this whole province ... Don Pedro Duque took great interest in enabling us to get all possible information about the little-known region into which we proposed to penetrate. Born in Colombia, but long a resident in Perú, he was a gentleman of the old school, keenly interested, not only in the administration and economic progress of his plantation, but in the intellectual movements of the outside world.... Our host was so energetic that as a result of his efforts a number of the best-informed residents were brought to the conferences at the great plantation house."

Bingham was an authority on the Inca civilization and, owing to this encounter with Señor Duque, would be credited with the rediscovery of Machu Picchu: "Don Pedro told us that in 1902 Lopez Torres, who had traveled much in the *montaña* [the "high jungle" in the eastern foothills of the Andes] looking for rubber trees, reported the discovery there of the ruins of an Inca city. All of Don Pedro's friends assured us that Conservidayoc was a terrible place to reach. 'No one living had been there.' 'It was inhabited by savage Indians who would not let strangers enter their village.'"

The Urubamba flows around the peaks of Machu Picchu on three sides, creating a virtual island isolated from roads and enclosed by stone cliffs and towering cloud forest. The route Williams and Orton wandered on foot from Ollantaytambo to Santa Ana would have taken them within miles of the lost Inca citadel. Four years later, Bingham, undaunted and determined, made the climb and beheld the ruins of Machu Picchu.

20. While *peon* is considered a derogatory term nowadays, it was commonly used in South America to identify the native laborer. In Perú, according to Yale geographer Isaiah Bowman in 1912, peóns were the

Indians of the agricultural plateau, as distinguished from the hunter-gatherer *savages* of the lower forests. Peóns were traditionally farmers and herdsmen, but owing to the lack of laborers, were forced into what Bowman describes as a "system more insidious than slavery," becoming increasingly indebted to their masters, the *patróns*.

The Indians of Perú's lowland forests were commonly called *savages*. Unlike the compliant peóns, they were independent and self-reliant, and not necessarily brutal or aggressive in behavior. It was the white man's savagery that forced the native Indians into dependence and slavery.

21. Echarate appears on an 1852 map of Perú. Owned by Braulio Polo, Hacienda Echarate was on the bank of the Urubamba about 15 miles north of Santa Ana. Isaiah Bowman of the Yale Peruvian Expedition wrote that Echarate was "where the heat becomes more intense and the first patches of tropical forest begin."

22. Surveyed in 1767, the Mason-Dixon line was regarded as the un-official border between the northern and southern states. Williams was born and reared in the deep South during its era of reconstruction, a time when vestiges of plantation life were inescapable. His mother was from a farming family that owned three slave families in 1860.

23. This is Williams's first mention of rubber, which was then Perú's most valuable natural resource. Made from latex, a sticky fluid drained from the Pará rubber tree indigenous only to the forests of the Amazon basin, it was first called *rubber* in 18th-century England, when it was demonstrated as effective in rubbing away pencil marks. But its useful-ness didn't end there. In the last half of the 19th century, there was an enormous demand for "injun rubber" as a water-resistant coating. It was, however, the invention of the automobile with its rubber tires that fueled the rush to harvest rubber from the Amazon basin.

"Rubber camps" were established at regular intervals along the Lower Urubamba, points where rubber gathered from the forests was transferred to canoes and launches that took it downriver to Iquitos. Some of these sites were temporary, their names now lost to history, while others be-came settlements and port towns.

The rubber boom in Perú lasted from 1870 to 1918, ending as suddenly as it had begun, when British entrepreneurs, using illicitly exported seeds, established more accessible rubber plantations in Ceylon and India.

24. Sahuayaco is a remote village ten miles northeast of Echarate and several miles north of the Urubamba.

25. The Yavero District is the densely forested area through which the Yavero River flows into the Urubamba.

26. Rosalina lies on the west bank of the Urubamba, about 20 miles downstream from Echarate. It was the point where the Urubamba became navigable by canoe. From his 1911 visit, Bowman, the Yale geographer, described it as "the last outpost of the valley settlements... hardly more than a name on the map and a camp site on the river bank," but maps show the Rosalina settlement in the hills overlooking the river.

27. *Yanatil* is a Quechua word, translated "black thick."

28. Castilian Spanish originated in northern and central Spain. It is the language of Buenos Aires, and its pronunciation varies distinctly from Lain American Spanish. Williams had resided in the Argentine capital for nine months, time enough to develop some facility with the language.

29. The chief offered the use of his canoes only as far as the Pongo Rapids for good reason: Even the sturdiest dugout canoes and rafts weren't built to bear up to the obstacles and violent rush of water they would encounter there. Destruction and death were thought to be almost certain. The Machiguenga Indians also revered the canyon as a sacred place inhabited by the souls of their dead.

30. Bowman of the Yale expedition wrote in 1912: "Señor Gonzales, the present owner of Hacienda Suhayco, recently obtained his land—a princely estate, ten miles by forty—for 12,000 soles ($6,000). In a few years he has cleared the best tract, built several miles of canals, hewed out houses and furniture, planted coca, cacao, cane, coffee, rice, pepper, and cotton and would not sell for $50,000. Moreover, instead of being a superintendent on a neighboring estate and keeping a shop in Cuzco where his large family was a source of great expense, he has become a wealthy landowner. He has educated a son in the United States. He is importing machinery, such as a rice thresher and a distilling plant. His son is looking forward to the purchase of still more playa land down river. He pays a sol a day to each laborer, securing men from Cotabambas and Abancay, where there are many Indians, a low standard of wages, little unoccupied land, and a hot climate, so that the immigrants do not need to become acclimated." (*Playa* refers to rich farmland that lies in a flood plain.)

31. Williams refers to the New Testament parable (Luke 16:19–31) in which the homeless beggar Lazarus lived outside the home of a wealthy man. When both men died, the beggar was taken to heaven, where he

stood with the prophet Abraham, while the rich man was sent to Hades to be tormented by fire. Looking up to Heaven, he begs Abraham to send Lazarus to "dip the tip of his finger in water and cool my tongue," but to no avail.

32. This was Convento Santo Domingo in Buenos Aires. It was completed in 1805, a year before British troops attacked the unfortified city. Captain Santiago de Liniers promised the church that if he received the protection of the Virgin and rousted the invaders, he would donate their colors to Convento Santo Domingo. Liniers was victorious and gave the flags to the church, where they are still kept.

33. *Wooden nutmeg* is a term for "anything false or fraudulent." It dates from 1829 when nutmeg was a rare and valuable commodity and Connecticut peddlers were said to have defrauded their customers by scattering fake nutmegs carved from wood in batches of real ones. Connecticut is sometimes identified as the Nutmeg State.

Chapter 5

1. The red brocket is a deer native to the forests of South America.

2. Williams's references to the "main river" throughout his text are to the Urubamba River.

3. The Andean spectacled bear is the only bear native to South America. It is smaller than North American bears and has a rounded face with a short muzzle, pale markings and a racoon-like mask. Primarily herbivores, they dwell in trees and tend to avoid people.

4. This is Williams's first mention of yuca, which would become the staple of his diet throughout the expedition. Yuca, pronounced YOO-ka and better known as cassava, is a woody shrub that grows in tropical climates. (It shouldn't be confused with the yucca plant common in North American landscaping.) The long, tapered yuca root is rich in carbohydrates and can be prepared and consumed much like a potato.

5. The sol was a Peruvian dollar, then worth about forty-eight cents.

6. The Yavero River is a stream that flows westward and enters the Urubamba south of the Pongo de Mainique.

7. Largely uninhabited and unmapped in 1907, Madre de Dios is a vast region of dense, low-lying rainforest northeast of Cuzco. It borders Brasil, Bolivia and the Peruvian regions of Puno, Cuzco and Ucayali. Its potential as a source for rubber and other agricultural products had been hampered by its isolation and the absence of navigable water-

ways to connect it with the Urubamba. *See Chapter 8, Note 5.*

8. The almost 400 species and subspecies of ants in Perú are the principal herbivores of Amazon basin forests. What Williams calls "coque ants" were large, broad-headed leaf eaters identified today as *cuki*.

9. The jaguar *(Panthera onca)* is the most powerful predator of the Americas. It tops the food chain in the jungles of Perú.

10. This was the language of the Machiguenga, the primary tribe occupying the forests surrounding the Pongo de Mainique.

Chapter 6

1. Williams was intrigued by the mysterious Señor Pereira, and his casual description of his host as "a petty ruler [living] with his forest children" was accurate. Williams and Orton are the earliest known English-speaking adventurers to visit the Pereira compound. In later years, three others reported on the old Spaniard and his ancestors.

In *The Andes of Southern Peru* (1916), Isaiah Bowman related his visit to what he described as "an Indian settlement and plantation owned by Pereira." He goes on to say: "Senor Pereira has gathered about him a group of Machigangas, and by marrying into the tribe has attained a position of great influence among the Indians. Upon our arrival a gun was fired to announce to his people that strangers had come, upon which the Machigangas strolled along in twos and threes from their huts, helped us ashore with the baggage, and prepared the evening meal."

Eighteen years later, Stratford D. Jolly, an Englishman, would enjoy the hospitality of Fidel Pereira, the old Spaniard's son. In his book, *The Treasure Trail* (1934), he reveals the elder Pereira's fate: "Señor Pereyra [the son, Fidel] we found to be a kindly, courteous man of forty-five, who made us most welcome. His father, a Spaniard, married a Machiguenga woman of whom he is the son. Years ago, in a quarrel, he was unfortunate enough to kill his father, and this unhappy event gave him a bad name and has made him shun the haunts of civilized men ever since. He has taken Machiguenga wives, by one of whom he has two sons, boys of fourteen and eleven years of age. They are gentle and refined, and have manners that many European children might copy with advantage."

In 1961, American naturalist and author Peter Matthiessen wrote of his own encounter with the Pereira clan in *The Cloud Forest*. He describes the then elderly Fidel Pereira as a fugitive ruler: "There, in a wilderness to which he held no title, he has established a huge domain, and has gained control of virtually all of his mother's people above the Pongo, even the wild Machiguengas of the tributary rivers. The law has not cared to follow Pereira into Pangoa, as his home grounds are known, and Pereira himself, a single visit to Quillabamba excepted, has not left the jungle in nearly forty years."

Years and decades apart, all four expeditions were following the Urubamba from Cuzco, and each one came to a halt as they neared the Pongo Rapids. It was only through the assistance of Señor Pereira and his descendants that each of these journeys continued safely past the churning rapids of the Pongo de Mainique.

2. The stream that Williams calls Río Sanriato is most likely Siriato, a stream that flows westward into the Urubama three miles south of Pongo de Mainique. It is easily confused with *Saniriato,* which a 1911 German map shows as a settlement just north of Pongo de Mainique.

3. Río Guayato is unidentifiable.

4. Current maps show Malanquiato as a village on the Urubamba about 12 miles north of the Pongo de Mainique, as Williams indicated.

5. A wickiup is a primitive frame hut covered with matting woven from palm fronds. Easily constructed and disassembled, it suited the needs of nomadic tribes. The term is associated with native American tribes of North America.

6. What are known as the Pongo Rapids flow through Pongo de Mainique, a canyon fifty yards wide and two miles long, with rock cliffs as much as half a mile in height. It's the only break in the Vilcabamba mountain range. Waterfalls cascade from its walls, further feeding the rushing waters of the Urubamba, and the Pongo Rapids are considered the most dangerous stretch of navigable river in the entire Amazonian system. Hazardous at any time of year, the waterway is especially treacherous during the rainy season. Isaiah Bowman, the Yale geographer wrote: "Once within its walls the Pongo offers small chance of escape."

The six square miles of rainforest surrounding the canyon are said to contain more living species than any other similar-sized area on Earth.

After rafting through the Pongo de Mainique in the late 1950s, Matthiessen was struck by the abrupt change in the Urubamba's surrounding landscape: "The mountain valleys and shadows have disappeared, replaced by the flat *selva,* which stretches away indefinitely behind red, eroding banks. The swift white streams plunging into the river are gone too; in their place are quiet creeks and shady leads." (*Selva* is land covered by dense equatorial forest.)

7. *Cauchero* is the Spanish word for a rubber gatherer, *caucho* being the fluid extracted from the rubber tree.

8. As described by Bowman of the Yale expedition, Puerto Mainique was a port on the Urubamba "just below the rapids" where a rubber company, the Compañia Gomera de Mainique, operated.

9. Below the Pongo Rapids, the desertion by Indian guides was not uncommon. They disappeared into the forest rather than risk being captured by slave traders at the next settlement.

10. *Head of navigation* is the farthest point above the mouth of a river that can be navigated by ships.

11. *Balsa* is not the name of the tree, but the Spanish word for "raft." The tree is the ochrona, which grows quickly and can reach a height of 100 ft. Ochrona timber is low in density and high in strength.

12. The advantage of a raft is its open construction; invading water washes over and between the timbers rather than accumulating, causing it to sink. The disadvantage of a raft is that it cannot be poled upstream; it's at the mercy of the downstream current and difficult to guide through rapids and whirlpools.

The lightweight ochrona logs stripped of their green bark are barely able to float. Buoyancy is achieved by allowing them to dry. The raft Williams and Orton built would have benefited from more than two days of drying—balsa wood sold today has been kiln dried for two weeks. The tendency of the wood to absorb water accounts for their raft becoming heavier and less buoyant over time. The vines known as lianas that are used to tie the timbers together are flexible and as strong as wood. Williams mentions a mooring vine attached to the raft for pulling it ashore. Vines were also used for lashing their belongings to the deck and may have been strung along the sides to serve as handholds.

Peruvian rafts have been constructed, just as Williams describes, since ancient times. Their seaworthiness was first documented when Pizarro's expedition encountered a trading *balsa* off the coast of Ecuador in 1526 and confirmed by Heyerdahl's *Kon-Tiki* voyage to Polynesia in 1954.

13. *Ague* refers to a feverish condition marked by chills and sweating that recur at regular intervals. These are symptoms of malaria.

14. *Portage* is carrying a boat overland around an obstacle.

15. Known in the Amazon basin as *remolinos,* whirlpools occur where

opposing currents meet. Williams's experience may sound exaggerated, but in *The Cloud Forest,* Matthiessen writes "Andrés has been on a *balsa* that was stuck in a large remolino for sixteen hours, and there is a known case of a *balsa* and crew caught in one for twenty-four days."

Chapter 7

1. The banana Williams speaks of is most likely a type of plantain, which contains more starch and less sugar than the sweet banana familiar to North Americans. In Perú, green and yellow plantains, peeled or un-peeled, are cooked or fried, as well as eaten raw.

2. Ritualistic cannibalism has been documented in the Amazon basin as late as the early twentieth century.

3. This was most likely malaria.

4. The ronsoco (or capybara) is not a hog, but the largest rodent in the world. Related to the guinea pig, it can reach two feet in height.

5. Mishahua was a rubber camp located near where the Mishahua River flows westward from the Madre de Dios into the Urubamba.

6. *Paroquets* refers to numerous species of small parrots (parakeets).

7. The grisly story recounted by Williams, one of "a fair sample of the many," was most likely untrue and circulated to instill fear, discouraging outsiders from entering tribal territories. In *Turn Right at Machu Picchu* (Penguin Random House, 2011), Mark Adams writes, "Reports claimed that the Antis were not merely cannibals but would slice pieces of flesh off their prey like sushimi, allowing the victim to witness himself being eaten alive. The tales were false, but as I'd learned ... the mischievous twins of Superstition and Legend tended to thrive in the Andes."

Chapter 8

1. The Shipibo-Conibo are an indigenous people who live along the Ucayali River. They had been the object of Christian missionary conver-sion efforts since the late 17th century. Peter Matthiessen provides a 20th-century description: "The Conibos are very colorful, with intricate black face marks, blue dye on the hands, elaborate bracelets of beads and wild animal teeth, and metal ornaments in the nose; the women also wear a long pendant of metal pierced through the lower lip."

2. Delirium tremens (or d.t.'s) are the rapid onset of confusion usually stemming from the withdrawal from alcohol.

3. Madre de Dios: *See Chapter 5, Note 7.*

4. Sepahua lies on the east bank of the Urubamba less than 15 miles from Mishahua. It's described by a traveler today as "a ramshackle town on the edge of Perú's Amazon jungle, nestled in a pocket on the map where a river of the same name flows into the Urubamba."
Mapping of the Urubamba was unreliable. Most maps published in the 1890s showed the port of Santa Rosa a considerable distance south of its actual location, an error that would be repeated by cartographers over the next two decades before Santa Rosa disappeared from maps.

5. There is a precedent to Señor Hosh's story of a steamboat being transported overland into the Madre de Dios by Indian slave labor. In the early 1890s, the notorious Peruvian rubber baron Carlos Fitzcarrald (1862-97) developed a route through that remote area between the Manú and Mishahua rivers that would allow rubber to be transported via the Urubamba, Ucayali and Amazon rivers to Atlantic ports. His determination to exploit the untapped rubber of the Madre de Dios led him to dismantle a 30-ton steamship, the *Contamana,* and transport it piece by piece across the isthmus separating the Mishahua and Manú rivers, an incredible task accomplished by the forced labor, under pain of death, of supposedly a thousand Indians. Ironically, Fitzcarrald drowned when the *Contamana* sank only a few years later.

6. Cumaria was a port town on the Ucayali, located at the mouth of the Coengua River. It first appeared on an 1892 map as Canaria.

7. The Amahuaca tribe of the southeastern Amazon basin had remained isolated until the 18th century and continued to resist assimilation. In 1961, Peter Matthiessen described them as "wild." They are currently under threat from ecological devastation, disease and violence brought by oil extractors and illegal loggers. In 1998 they numbered only about 520. According to Matthiessen, "In South America, with few exceptions, the tribe which permits itself to come into complete contact with the white man, on the white man's terms, has perhaps a half-century of existence left to it."

8. Rayas are venomous freshwater stingrays.

9. A snag is a fallen tree or limb that has become firmly implanted in the sediment in the bed of a stream, creating a hazard to navigation.

10. Slave laborers were first brought to Perú from China in the early 1600s. One hundred thousand contract laborers, mostly male, arrived from Asia between 1849 and 1874, most of them to work on sugar plantations. Many adopted the surname of their patrón. Although Williams

uses the now-derogatory term *Chinaman,* the country's Asian population also represented Japan and the Philippines.

11. On the west bank of the Tambo River close to its mouth, Misión Santa Rosa de los Piros had been founded by Jesuit missionaries, who dedicated the surrounding area to the cultivation of cotton. The community that developed around the mission was also known as Buena Vista until 1928 when it became Atalaya. A bustling town today, Atalaya marks the confluence of the cold, brown Tambo from the western highlands and the warm, green Urubamba from the jungle. Together they form the Ucayali River. Their waters resist mixing, so the 1,100-mile Ucayali begins as one river with two colors and temperatures.

12. The birds that Williams mentions are unidentifiable by the Quechua names he gives them. The number and diversity of birds in the Amazon basin is extraordinary, with new species continually being discovered in its forests. Well over 1,700 species (close to 20 percent of the world's total) have been registered.

13. The bufeo is a fresh-water dolphin found throughout the Amazon basin; it grows pink in color as it ages. The giant river otter is a type of weasel that lives in the rivers and creeks of the Amazon river system and said to grow as long as six feet.

14. The Inuya River is a tributary of the Urubamba, flowing westward about 25 miles upstream from Santa Rosa (present-day Atalaya).

Chapter 9

1. What Williams calls a *cacho* was most likely *Choco tinamou,* a bird that lays its eggs on the ground in dense growth or among the exposed roots of trees.

2. Alto Ucayali is the upper Ucayali River, which continues northward over a course of 995 miles before entering the Amazon River. The Apurímac River begins as glacial meltwater at an elevation of 18,360 ft. in the Andes west of Cusco. As it flows downward—a distance of 675 miles—it becomes the Ene and Tambo rivers before meeting the Urubamba to form the Ucayali. A tributary of the Apurímac is said to be the farthermost source of the Amazon River.

3. The Campa Indians, also known as the Asháninkas, are one of the great warrior tribes of the eastern foothills of the Andes. Following a violent dispute with a Franciscan mission in 1925, they moved deep into the jungles to escape the Peruvian military. In *The Cloud Forest,* Matthies-

sen described them as having "faces heavily painted with the orange of the achote berry." In the 21st century, they remain relatively isolated and have little to do with the cash economy, preferring to live by subsistence agriculture, hunting and fishing

4. The French expedition was mapping the territory for a corporation engaged in the export of rubber. As Williams describes it, the expedition was headed by a director-general with the American engineer serving as director. Williams fails to identify the American, the corporation or any member of the French expedition by name.

5. The slave post Logoto appears as *Largoto* on a map by a German cartographer from 1922. He places it north of Santa Rosa on the opposite shore of the Ucayali. Its being situated on the eastern bank greatly reduced the possibility of escape.

6. The Gran Pajonal, translated "great grassland," is a rugged plateau area west of Santa Rosa and continuing to the foothills of the Andes. It is heavily clouded with low, dense forests of very high biodiversity, but without navigable waterways, only rapid, white-water streams. Its 4,000 square miles are sparsely inhabited by native Indians, primarily the Asháninka tribe.

7. Shown on maps of Perú between 1852 and 1931, Vuelta del Diablo is a 12 ft. deep strait on the Ucayali River north of the confluence of the Urubamba and Tambo rivers. Many of these maps warned "The Ucayali is navigable [southward from the Amazon] for large vessels to this place." An 1850 expedition provided this description: "The current dashes with much violence against the trunks of large trees which lodge in, and almost block up, its passage."

8. *Manta blanca* (translated "white cloak") are biting midges that travel in swarms in the daytime. They are known to transmit several diseases.

9. Williams may have confused what he called nigritte herons with nigritas, a bird he would have recalled from his years in South Africa, but which is not found in the Americas. Garza rosada is a wading bird of the ibis and spoonbill family, common east of the Andes and prized for its pink feathers.

10. What Williams calls the Curahuanta River is possibly the Coenhua River, which flows westward into the Ucayali at Cumaria.

11. The narrow passage that Williams calls Shebaya Pass is unidentifiable by that name today.

12. In 1871, Henry Morton Stanley, a correspondent for the *New York*

Herald, headed an expedition into East Africa in search of Dr. David Livingstone, a British missionary-explorer who had been missing for six years. Stanley's dispatches made sensational news, and after finding Livingstone, he became known far and wide as the consummate explorer.

Chapter 10

1. It was only after rubber trees began to be harvested in this remote territory that the exact borders between Perú and the Brasilian states of Amazonas and Acre came into question. The conflict could only be resolved by accurately mapping the heavily forested, scarcely populated border: five hundred twisting miles of the Yavarí River, from its source in the Ucayali highlands to its mouth on the Amazon.

2. The atrocities that Williams reports were far more severe than he witnessed. In 1910. the British government launched an earnest investigation that accomplished little more than confirming the abuse. One year later, Isaiah Bowman of the Yale expedition wrote: "What a story it could tell if a ball of smoke-cured rubber on a New York dock were endowed with speech—of the wet jungle path, of enslaved peóns, of vile abuses by immoral agents, of all the toil and sickness that make the tropical lowland a reproach!" Peter Matthiessen, in the *The Cloud Forest,* wrote, "Someone has estimated that the number of Indians butchered in the few decades of the rubber boom exceeded all the lives lost in World War I—this figure entirely apart from the thousands who died in slavery."

3. Tahuanía was a settlement on the Ucayali near present-day Bolognesi.

4. *Punting* refers to the use of a pole to drive a vessel through water.

Chapter 11

1. The Unini River enters the Ucayali from the west about 12 miles north of Santa Rosa (present-day Atalaya).

2. Climbing irons were a pair of spiked iron frames designed to be strapped to boots or the lower legs to provide traction when climbing trees or slopes.

3. These were three of the indigenous tribes of this remote area of the Amazon rainforest. In 1998, the estimated population of the Mashco-Piro had dwindled to between 100 and 250.

4. Unidentifiable as the name of a bird, *tontaco* is translated from colloquial Spanish as "fool" and used as an insult.

5. Snake stones are a common folk remedy for snake bites in Africa,

South America and Asia. In Perú, a black stone (often only a small charred animal bone) is applied to the site of a poisonous bite, tied firmly in place and left for several days, during which time it supposedly draws the venom from the wound. Potassium permanganate is an inorganic chemical compound. As a medication it is used for cleaning wounds and fungal infections. In 1904, it was proven effective in treating snake bites when used with a knife-like device, but useless when applied with a hypodermic syringe.

6. The Sapani is a stream that originates in the Gran Pajonal about twelve miles west of Santa Rosa and winds its way to the Ucayali.

7. Although the French expedition could well have been the first to make a trek from the Upper Ucayali through that particular area of the Gran Pajonal, they had been preceded as early as 1595 by Jesuit missionaries known to have made contact with Ashaninka tribesmen, as well as by various military expeditions from Lima during the colonial period. More recently, in the 1890s, Father Sala, a Franciscan priest, led two armed expeditions through the Gran Pajonal. His report to the Peruvian government demonstrates an evil-minded, conspiratorial approach to ministry: "Through terror and moderate punishments, [the Indians] will feel obliged to throw themselves at the mercy of the missionary father, and he in turn will be able, with great charity and prudence to exercise his divine ministrations on those unfortunate creatures.... Once a rubber boss has subjugated the ferocious Indian at gunpoint, the time will be opportune for the missionary father to immediately step in and offer him the services and consolations of our Holy Religion."

Chapter 12

1. *The Life and Adventures of Martin Chuzzlewit* by Charles Dickens was first published in the 1840s.

2. Williams's family in Alabama knew that he was traveling through South America. Up until he left Cuzco, he had kept in touch by sending them picture postcards.

3. Masisea is a village on the Ucayali, 320 nautical miles north of Santa Rosa, near present-day Pucallpa.

4. Communication by telegraph to and from the Amazon basin remained close to impossible in the early 1900s. In 1881, the *New York Times* had broken the news that telegraphic communication would soon be established between New York and Central and South America "by

direct wires, and that news and business advices will be as regularly and fully received from the countries on the west coast below the equator as they now are from Europe. The Central and South American Telegraph Company is pushing the construction of its land lines and laying its submarine cables as rapidly as the wires can be supplied." It would, however, take decades to connect with remote inland locales like Iquitos, and maintaining the cable lines would be an ongoing challenge.

5. Bordering Perú, Mato Grosso is an inland state in western Brasil. Its terrain varies from wetlands and woods to savanna plains. In the early twentieth century, explorers arrived there in search of precious metals as well as lost civilizations.

Chapter 13

1. Attempts to capture color images had been ongoing for decades. The European physicist Gabriel Lippmann invented a photographic method that reproduced colors, based on light-wave interference. It was enough to earn him the Nobel Prize in Physics for 1908.

In late 1907, owing to increasing tension in American-Japanese relations, President Theodore Roosevelt ordered the transfer of the Navy's Atlantic fleet of sixteen white-painted battleships to the Pacific. What began as a show of force became a goodwill tour of the "Great White Fleet" that circumnavigated the globe, paying friendly visits to key countries while, at the same time, displaying American military might.

2. *Caramba* is a Spanish interjection often used to express surprise.

3. Pará: *See Chapter 14, Note 5.*

4. *Cordillera* is the Spanish word for "mountain range."

5. At the port of Iquitos, 2,500 miles from the Atlantic Ocean, the Ucayali becomes the Amazon River. In the late 1800s, the Anglo-Peruvian Amazon Co. was established in Iquitos, making it the center of rubber export from the Amazon basin. The rubber boom attracted thousands of European traders to Iquitos, where they amassed considerable wealth, while the indigenous workers lived in near slavery conditions forcefully imposed by the British company. By 1900, the city's population had grown to 20,000. In the 21st century, Iquitos, with a population of a half million, remains the capital of the Peruvian Amazon, although it still cannot be reached by road.

6. The barbasco plant is a type of aloe. Matthiessen described this method of fishing as practiced in the late 1950s: "They destroy many

more fish than they can use by grinding the barbasco plant in the bottom of a dugout, which is then overturned in a lake or stream. The poisonous barbasco—the source of rotenone, used in insecticides—litters the surface with dead and dying creatures. The practice is against the law, but again, the law is all but unenforceable."

Chapter 14

1. *Ship a wave* is an expression meaning to take in water over the side of a vessel.

2. Built in Aberdeen, Scotland, the steamship *Huayna* was launched from Liverpool, England, by the Booth Steamship Co. in 1893 as the SS *Hildebrand*. Built of steel, it was 261 feet long. In 1908, it was transferred to the Iquitos Steamship Co., Liverpool, England, and renamed *Huayna*. (Huayna Capac was the eleventh Inca emperor.) It served the British Navy during World War I.

3. Beriberi is a disease caused by the deficiency of vitamin B-1.

4. Generally known as Río Amazonas in Spanish and Portuguese, the Amazon River is more than 4,000 miles long from its headwaters in Perú to its mouth on Brasil's Atlantic coast. The distance by air from Iquitos to the Atlantic is roughly 1,500 miles, but the journey by boat is 2,300 miles. Twenty percent of the water flowing into the world's oceans is discharged by the Amazon.

5. Manaós, Brasil, located at the confluence of the Negro River with the Amazon, was at the center of the rubber boom of the late 1800s. The wealth and extravagance of the rubber barons made it a gaudy spectacle of wide avenues, plazas and grand public buildings. In 1897, the domed opera house opened with a performance by the Italian tenor Enrico Caruso. But the days were numbered for this "Paris of the Tropics"; it was all but abandoned when the rubber boom came to an abrupt end.

6. Pará (known today as Belém) is the gateway to the Amazon. A deep-water port, it lies on the Pará River, 925 miles from Manaós and about sixty miles upriver from the Atlantic Ocean. In 1908, it was the main export center of the rubber industry.

7. Lee English Williams was one of two passengers added to the manifest of the British Booth Line's SS *Cuthbert* when it sailed from Pará on August 10, 1908. It arrived at the Port of New York twelve days later.

Bingham, Hiram, *Machu Picchu, A Citadel of the Incas: Report of the Explorations and Excavations Made in 1911, 1912 and 1915 under the Auspices of Yale University and the National Geographic Society,* Oxford University Press, 1930.

—, *Inca Land: Explorations in the Highlands of Peru,* National Geographic, Washington D.C., 2003.

—, *Lost City of the Incas: The Story of Machu Picchu and Its Builders,* Weidenfield and Nicholson, London, 2002.

Bowman, Isaiah, "The Cañon of the Urubamba," *Bulletin of the American Geographical Society,* Vol. 44, No. 12, 1912.

—, *The Andes of Southern Peru: Geographical Reconnaissance Along the Seventy-Third Meridian,* American Geographical Society of New York, Holt, New York, 1916.

Dyott, G.M., *Silent Highways of the Jungle,* Chapman & Dodd. Ltd., London, 1924.

Farabee, William Curtis, *Indian Tribes of Eastern Peru,* Peabody Museum of Archaeology and Ethnology, Harvard University, Cambridge, Mass., 1922.

Frank, Harry Alverson, *Vagabonding Down the Andes,* Century, New York, 1917.

Gade, Daniel W., *Spell of the Urubamba: Anthropogeographical Essays on an Andean Valley in Space and Time,* Springer, Berlin, 2015.

Garland, Alejandro, *Peru in 1906 and After,* La Industria Printing Office, Lima, 1908.

Gibbon, Lardner, *Exploration of the Valley of the Amazon Made Under the Direction of the Navy Department, Volume II,* Robert Armstrong Public Printer, Washington, 1853.

Jolly, Stratford D., *The Treasure Trail: Some Adventures,* John Long, London, 1934.

Marcoy, Paul, *Travels in South America, From the Pacific Ocean to the Atlantic Ocean,* Scribner, Armstrong & Co., New York, 1875.

Markham, Clements R., *Expeditions into the Valley of the Amazon, 1539, 1540, 1639,* Hakluyt Society, London, 1859.

Matthiessen, Peter, *The Cloud Forest: A Chronicle of the South American Wilderness,* Viking Press, New York, 1961.

Smith, Anthony, *Explorers of the Amazon,* University of Chicago Press, Chicago, 1994.

This is Lee English Williams's story. He lived it with the courage born out of necessity—and lived to write about it. What he wrote with such wonder was the treasure in the attic, waiting to be discovered only because my great grandfather, grandmother, mother and brother let it be.

I'm grateful to many people who helped turn three newspaper tear sheets into this book. From the beginning, the encouragement of Marta Mitchell Strait, my cousin and a great niece of the author has been a blessing. In New Orleans, John Church and John Hall provided warm hospitality and steered me to the Historic New Orleans Collection on Royal Street, where the staff of helpful librarians and the complete *Times-Democrat* text were waiting.

The first readers were Jude Goodier-Mojher, Pam Utz, Ann Spivack and Gary Jones. I'm beyond grateful for their extensive notes, questions and suggestions, as well as for their enthusiasm. Pam, through her friend Penny Berliner, put me in touch with Keith Muscutt, an archaeologist and present-day explorer of Perú's eastern Andean rain forest, who generously shared his insight and advice.

Michael Mojher created the book's beautiful cover. We go way back, and my appreciation of his artistry and judgment remains boundless. Gary Jones, my right-hand man in most everything, also assisted with the mapmaking.

Thanks to the resources available on the Internet, I was able to locate the most obscure supportive documents, read the accounts of other expeditions into the Amazon basin and trace Williams's journey on dozens of century-old maps as well as by satellite.

Nevertheless, there are questions that remain unanswered. Who was James Orton? What became of Lee Williams? Who knows?

—Don Roberts